Pecan America

Pecan America

Exploring a Cultural Icon

John Gifford

UNIVERSITY PRESS OF KANSAS

Photos by John Gifford.

Material from this book originally appeared in *Modern Farmer.*

Published by the University Press of Kansas (Lawrence, Kansas 66045), which was organized by the Kansas Board of Regents and is operated and funded by Emporia State University, Fort Hays State University, Kansas State University, Pittsburg State University, the University of Kansas, and Wichita State University.

Library of Congress Cataloging-in-Publication Data
Names: Gifford, John, author.
Title: Pecan America : exploring a cultural icon / John Gifford.
Description: Lawrence : University Press of Kansas, [2019] |
Includes bibliographical references.
Identifiers: LCCN 2019006699
ISBN 9780700628353 (cloth : alk. paper)
ISBN 9780700628360 (ebook)
Subjects: LCSH: Pecan—Growth—United States. | Pecan—Nutrition.
Classification: LCC SB401.P4 G54 2019 | DDC 634/.52—dc23
LC record available at https://lccn.loc.gov/2019006699.

British Library Cataloguing-in-Publication Data is available.

Printed in the United States of America

10 9 8 7 6 5 4 3 2 1

The paper used in this publication is recycled and contains 30 percent postconsumer waste. It is acid free and meets the minimum requirements of the American National Standard for Permanence of Paper for Printed Library Materials Z39.48-1992.

For Jackson

Contents

Introduction

At the time I began my research for this book, in 2016, I knew precious little about pecans or pecan trees. What I had was a general understanding of nature and ecology, an extremely limited and dated background in small-scale agriculture, but perhaps most importantly, an interest in learning and a process, honed through twenty years spent working as a freelance writer, of immersing myself in worlds I knew little or nothing about so that I might eventually learn enough to write something of value for others to read. My interest in pecans at this point was limited to a single tree. Somewhere I'd heard about Oklahoma's champion pecan, and wanting to see this grand old tree, drove two hours from my home in Oklahoma City to the Tishomingo National Wildlife Refuge in Johnston County, near the Red River, where pecans grow in abundance as they have for thousands of years. Upon my arrival I was amazed to discover much of the refuge in flood stage, including the vast river-bottom field surrounding the champion pecan. When I inquired with refuge officials, I was told there was no way to get out to the tree. The water was too deep, they said, and the big pecan was inundated. It wasn't the first time, they told me. But, if I were patient, the flood waters would again recede as they had so often during the previous year of record-cracking deluges.

In the meantime there were other pecan trees to see and an entire industry that had been built around them. Initially, I intended to write only an essay on Oklahoma's champion pecan tree, but after shelling so much intriguing information on the botany and history, and on the health benefits and industry of pecans, and after meeting so many interesting people in my travels throughout the US pecan belt, and upon learning that the pecan industry now finds itself at perhaps the most important point in its history, my essay turned into a book.

In researching pecans, one of the first things I discovered was that growers, shellers, scientists, and even retailers, when referencing the trees, often distinguish them as being either cultivars (improved) or native (wild). This is particularly true for those industry stakeholders in states like Arkansas, Louisiana, Oklahoma, and Texas, where these trees are indigenous and where wild pecans continue to grow today. And the Oklahoma champion pecan, which I set out to see and experience in April 2016, and which spent nearly a year, off and on, submerged in floodwaters and thus elusive to me, was a native. Of this there could be no doubt, even from a distance. This enormous tree was fascinating, for its age was unknown, even to the officials of the Tishomingo National Wildlife Refuge, who had nominated it for recognition as the state's champion of the species. To me it was stately and majestic, a living window into the past and, perhaps most of all, a survivor. As I gazed out over the expansive lake separating it from me, I wondered how many floods this tree had endured over the past century or more.

Floods, I learned, were something that wild pecan trees have been surviving for millennia. It seems they're equipped for it, for they evolved along the central and southern portions of the Mississippi River and its many tributaries, where they were subjected to regular inundations of water and alluvial deposits. Yet, despite their ability to withstand and even benefit from temporary flooding, pecan trees are most prolific in those areas featuring well-drained soils. For this reason pecan growers are often advised to conduct percolation tests in areas designated for new plantings, whereby one digs a hole thirty or so inches in depth, fills it with water, and then monitors its drainage rate over the next forty-eight hours. As one pecan scientist explained at a recent industry seminar, ideally all the water will drain out, although a minimum of eighteen to twenty-four inches of drainage is suitable for pecans.

Given their evolution in areas blessed with abundant rainfall and moist soils, it's easy to understand how pecan trees have adapted to the climate of the southeast United States, where they've been introduced and have thrived for more than a century. What many find surprising, on the other hand, is that they've fared so well in the desert Southwest, where in some areas only twelve or fourteen inches of rain fall each year, compared with fifty inches or more in parts of the Southeast. Their cultivation in this parched corner of our nation is made possible, of course, through the miracle of irrigation and also by the development of cultivars especially suited to the pecan belt's western growing region.

The effort to domesticate pecans is in many ways still in its infancy. Even the pecan industry itself is relatively new, barely a hundred years old. For these reasons, improved trees remain genetically similar to their wild counterparts. Yet the differences between the two are often significant and compelling, as is suggested by today's enormously successful pecan industry in places like Arizona and New Mexico. Although these states are outside the tree's native range, currently they account for some of our nation's most prolific pecan production. Indeed, the ongoing effort to develop new and better cultivars, varieties specially adapted to specific insect, disease, and environmental challenges, is at the heart of today's pecan industry. It's also one of the primary reasons why the pecan tree has fared so well in modern times. And this is inspiring, for in an age that all too often finds us lamenting the imperilment of one species or the loss of another, the pecan is one of our culture's success stories. Unlike much of our native flora and fauna, the pecan tree has thrived in the wake of human progress. Today pecans grow in every southern state, from the Carolinas to California. Yet the industry that has sprouted up around this highly adaptable crop is based largely on the cultivation of improved varieties, or cultivars, trees propagated by human hands rather than Mother Nature's. Cultivars are developed not only to withstand certain environmental challenges, but also for the production of nuts featuring some specific quality, such as larger, more easily shelled kernels, for example, which are more valuable in the marketplace. These improvements, however, come at the expense of genetic diversity and the type of hybrid vigor resulting from thousands of years of natural, pecan-tree evolution. This results in tree varieties that require a certain level of human management in order to produce the quality and quantity of nuts for which they've been developed, and to ensure the tree's long-term survival. Although this has fueled the expansion of the American pecan industry, it has complicated, at least for me, the very idea of the pecan as a food, as a cultural marker, and certainly as an agricultural crop.

In nature, every wild pecan tree is genetically unique. But as we have strived over the past century to produce trees (and ultimately pecans) with very specific qualities, we've continued to work our way toward an increasingly limited product, genetically speaking. While this strategy certainly mirrors the philosophy of consistency that any successful corporation strives to associate with its brand, it also begs a question: is the product produced through such narrowing parameters necessarily better? Or, in this case, is the "improved" pecan better than its natural counterpart? Are cultivated pecans somehow superior to natives? Or vice versa?

These questions were constantly on my mind as I began my research for this book. After all, they stemmed from a phenomenon that was being pointed out to me at what seemed every turn. A pecan tree, I was reminded again and again, was either natural (wild) or improved/domesticated (cultivated). Which was better? Which was best? Eventually I realized there was no easy answer, and I dismissed the notion of a superior pecan of any kind. While it's often said that native pecans contain a greater oil content, providing, perhaps, a flavor superior to their cultivated counterparts, pecan stakeholders in areas outside the nut's native range frequently disagree with this assessment, citing a lack of documented research on the subject. Thus, the best pecan may well be the one produced in the state where you're standing—or more specifically, the one grown, processed, or marketed by the pecan stakeholder with whom you're conversing. One presenter at a 1907 meeting of the Texas Nut Growers' Association distinguished between the consumer's and the producer's versions of an ideal pecan, noting that the former looks only to the nut, with no regard for the tree that produced it, while a farmer considers both the pecan and the tree. In describing the components of his perfect pecan, this presenter, H. A. Halbert of Coleman, Texas, noted such factors as color, flavor, shell, shape, and size, culminating, ideally for Halbert, in a pecan "weighing sixty to the pound, round in shape, the shell a mere film, which can be easily cracked in the palm of the hand, kernel easily cleaned and of sweetest flavor, nut of brown color with dashes of black at the apex."

Even a century ago pecan size was the chief selection criterion for many consumers. To a great extent this seems to have carried through to modern times. Shoppers continue to associate pecan size with quality, in many cases believing the larger the pecan, the better the flavor and greater still the health benefits. This is especially true of Chinese buyers who demand, and who are willing to pay the highest prices for, some of the larger pecan varieties, such as Desirable. Yet, one pecan grower told me recently, the only thing desirable about Desirable is the name. In other words, as with any other food, the idea of an ideal pecan is a subjective matter, varying from consumer to consumer. Among producers, preferred pecan varieties differ from one part of the country to another, influenced both by market demands and by what grows best in any given region. In the Southeast, it might be Schley or Elliott; in the Southwest, perhaps it's Wichita or Western Schley. In the South Central United States, where this nut evolved over millennia, native pecans are still an important part of the annual harvest, and many growers and consumers insist on them.

In years past and until recently, this has been a surprisingly divisive issue within the industry. Once, at a national pecan-industry gathering, I asked an insider if he thought native pecans were on their way out. Before replying, he quickly glanced over his shoulder, then lowered his voice and said, "John, there are people here who'd like to rip every wild pecan tree out of the ground and replace them with cultivars." The money, he said, was in these improved varieties, and that's where the industry was heading and had been for a long time. And it still is. But in recent years the US pecan industry is beginning to sense that perhaps cultivated and native pecans, and their producers and methodologies and visions, aren't mutually exclusive, that maybe there's acreage for both, and that their respective proponents, even in different regions of the country, can work better together.

Today, the pecan industry is on the cusp of becoming a truly unified organization with a like-minded constituency, or failing this, of remaining an entity of independent (and frequently disparate) concerns loosely affiliated around a specialty crop that just happens to have originated here in the United States and for which worldwide demand, at the moment, just happens to be exploding.

Seeking to benchmark some of the same strategies that have propelled the almond, walnut, and pistachio to top-of-mind awareness among consumers the world over, the pecan industry, in 2016, for the first time made the decision to work together to advance and elevate the industry surrounding America's indigenous tree nut through the implementation of a federal marketing order (FMO). This is a voluntary, USDA-approved, self-assessment providing funding for research, a governing body, and for the first time in the history of this aspiring industry, a concerted marketing effort with the goal of branding Texas pecans and Georgia pecans and New Mexico pecans and Mississippi pecans as a singular product: the American pecan. Many are wondering, can this industry, whose constituency has long shown a tendency for fierce independence, regional rivalries, even outright opposition, work together? More importantly, will this industry, which is based largely on cultivars, continue to devalue wild pecans?

That's not the scope of this book. After all, to answer these questions satisfactorily we would need to look many years into the future. But they're interesting to consider, nevertheless, and they're certainly on the mind of many of the pecan stakeholders I met and spoke to. What was on my mind as I researched for this project, especially after reading about the pecan's age-old and evolving story in books like James McWilliams's *The Pecan: A History of America's Native Nut*, and about pecan history and physiology and horticulture in Jane Manaster's *The Pecan Tree* and Lenny Wells's *Pecan: America's Native Nut Tree*, were questions surrounding the industry of what I've come to realize is an American treasure. I wanted to see and experience this industry for myself, an industry that has grown up around a tree that's both native and extremely abundant here on the southern Great Plains, in Oklahoma. I wanted to meet some of the people who produce, process, market, research, and otherwise help bring this intriguing food to our tables. I wanted to better understand the pecan's place in our culture. The Georgia Pecan Commission implores us to "think beyond the pie," for example, and I wanted to know just how far beyond it we've ventured. With scientific research continuing to reveal significant health benefits for those who consume pecans, with growers across the pecan belt planting thousands of acres of new trees to meet the increasing worldwide demand for this nut, and given the growing class of consumers who view the pecan as not just an everyday kitchen staple but as a premium food, even a luxury item, one needn't look beyond the price tag for pecans at his or her local supermarket to realize things are happening in this industry. Demand for pecans is increasing. And as consumer preferences continue to evolve, the pecan industry is working not only to meet them but also to help set certain expectations. How, I wondered, is an industry whose chief product, which has traditionally been viewed as a niche item for holidays or as a seasonal emblem of a certain region's culture, working to assert itself and, maybe more importantly, to differentiate itself, in a market segment whose branches are already bowing under the bumper-crop weight of such household names as almonds and walnuts? I traveled throughout the US pecan belt over a period of two years to find out. I talked to consumers, as well as pecan farmers, shellers, marketers, and researchers, who told me again and again that the pecan's (and the industry's) best days are just ahead.

Yet, for all the effort the pecan industry has made recently to assimilate and begin working together to produce and nurture and brand and market a singular generic product—something called the American pecan—it seems beset with a spirit of independence and freedom that is the very essence of America itself. And as I gradually understood this, I began to realize that this is no ordinary crop. For in the pecan we have America in a nutshell, a food that has seen our country at its best, and worst; one that sustained and nourished our land's earliest residents; one that was right here waiting, and had been for ages, when the first Europeans arrived on our shores; one enhanced by its inherent diversity; and one whose industry now finds itself at a defining moment in its history.

The pecan may be one of our most enigmatic crops, a food item many Americans read about in newspapers and culinary magazines each November and December, and which they enjoy in their holiday pies, but which they may not even consider, let alone eat, the rest of the year. As incredible as it may sound, there are still some of us who know next to nothing about pecans, who've never seen a pecan, who've never tasted a pecan, and who have no idea just how nutritious and healthful these antioxidant-rich tree nuts really are. Meanwhile, there is an entire industry working to change this. This book—not a history of the pecan, not a deep dive into pecan physiol-

The storefront of this abandoned building in Louisiana reminds us of the important role that pecans have traditionally played in many American communities, particularly in the South. As the planting of pecan trees has expanded across the United States in recent decades, this unique tree nut is playing an increasingly significant economic, cultural, and biologic role in a growing number of American communities and geographic regions.

ogy or horticulture, but rather, part travelogue, part exploration, and a celebration of an incredibly edible American treasure and the thriving culture surrounding it—showcases some of these individuals and the work they do in bringing an authentic taste of our beloved land to fellow Americans and to a growing number of consumers around the globe.

I should point out that *Pecan America* is not an academic exercise aimed at a scholarly or technical audience. This is a book written for general readers, especially those interested in discovering how deeply rooted pecans are in American culture. I have tried to give readers a more holistic view of my subject, not only in contrast to, but also to complement the outstanding information presented in the aforementioned titles. Consequently, *Pecan America* features writing on the history, botany, ecology, economy, industry, and health benefits of pecans as a way of better understanding this tree nut's place in our culture. Rather than limit my exploration of pecans to a single region or state, I traveled across the country to see for myself where they come from and how they're produced. One of the remarkable things I discovered was that, even among those who grow or market or consume this tree nut, we can't even agree on how to pronounce the word "pecan." But as John Mellencamp still sings, "Ain't that America?"

So many of the foods we eat here in the United States have their origins in other countries and in other parts of the world, but in the pecan we have something truly American, a supremely nutritious nut that sustained our earliest residents and that nourishes us today. And with consumers around the planet continuing to discover its delectable flavor, versatility, and growing suite of health benefits, we can take satisfaction in knowing that they're experiencing a little bit of America itself.

As one pecan researcher told me, we should be proud of this.

—1—

The Flood

All roads were leading me to water. And as much as I love the stuff, and though it's vital to life, I hadn't traveled to the Tishomingo National Wildlife Refuge in south-central Oklahoma for the water. What I wanted was terrestrial, a product of the surrounding river bottoms, and for more than a century a stalwart feature of the bucolic, southern Oklahoma landscape. But at every turn there was water.

This wasn't supposed to be the case. Though the refuge is home to Cumberland Pool—a shallow but vast freshwater "estuary," a part of Lake Texoma, supporting both resident and migrating birds, as well as fish and other wildlife—which encompasses one quarter of the park's 16,464 acres, most of the surrounding landscape should have been dry. And the week before, it was. But between the time I'd spoken with Joanne Ryan, the refuge's education specialist, and the day of my visit in late April, heavy rains had pummeled the area. Add to this an enormous log jam in the nearby Washita River—a US Fish & Wildlife Service representative told me it was a "half-mile long" and was certainly a product of the previous year's historic floods—and the result was a rapidly rising water table, which practically overnight had flooded fields and forests, inundating much of the refuge in water and reminding Tishomingo residents of the record rains of 2015, which had submerged two dozen homes and swamped most of the refuge's outbuildings, including its headquarters office. One year later Joanne and the other US Fish & Wildlife Service staff were still sharing a temporary office off-site, in Tishomingo, in a building the Chickasaw Nation had provided them rent free.

When I arrived and found much of the refuge under water, and my path to the wildlife observation deck flooded—I was told I could easily spot Oklahoma's champion pecan tree from this viewing platform—I phoned Joanne.

"We got a lot of rain," she said. "You can't get out there."

"I don't mind wading," I said. "I have to see this pecan tree."

"It's under five or six feet of water."

"Again?" I asked.

"Again," she said. "Unfortunately, we don't know how this will affect the tree."

This was problematic for many reasons, including the fact that in the previous year's record-setting flood, 90 percent of the Tishomingo National Wildlife Refuge was under water for forty-five days. Pecan trees evolved over the ages in the deep alluvial soil of the Mississippi River floodplain. As a result, they tolerate regular flooding, which nature has equipped them to survive. But the 2015 storms were historic; the year ended as the state's wettest on record. And no one, even refuge officials, even representatives from the Oklahoma Forestry Service, could say for certain how the unusually severe and prolonged flooding had impacted the health of the state's champion pecan tree, if at all.

To compound matters, some of southern Johnston County's largest and most significant trees had toppled and fallen to the ground as a result of the previous year's floods. The standing water had softened the soil so much that the earth was unable to support some of these seventy- and eighty-foot-tall trees, especially in the perpetual Oklahoma winds. Considering the amount of moisture in the soil,

I wondered whether the state's greatest pecan tree was consigned to a similar fate. No one knew, of course, and for me this was reason enough to get out to the Tishomingo National Wildlife Refuge and see this distinguished tree before it was too late. There was another problem, however.

Because the champion pecan is located in an area of the refuge that's closed to the public, I couldn't get out there on my own, even if it had been dry. And Justin, the biologist who had agreed way back when, a week earlier, when things were dry, to take me out to the tree, happened to be away that morning.

"But I have to see this tree," I told Joanne. "Is there anyone else who can take me out there?"

"Can you hold on a minute?" she said.

I climbed out of my car. Standing in the refuge's picnic area, listening to the spring symphony of birdsong all around me, absolutely enthralled by the meadow of lush native grasses and blooming Indian paintbrush and the contentment of busy pollinators at work—fluttering butterflies and buzzing bees—I felt my stress slowly but surely slipping away, despite my predicament. It occurred to me what a valuable gift our national parks and wildlife refuges are, and what a salubrious antidote to city life they provide.

When Joanne came back on the line, she said, "Our equipment operator said he would drive you out there."

"Wonderful!" I said. "Thank you."

"He's on his way," Joanne said.

Since the 1960s the Oklahoma Forestry Association, in partnership with Oklahoma Forestry Services, has searched for, measured, and maintained a list of the state's largest trees. The 2014 edition of *The Great Trees of Oklahoma* contains listings for nearly 100 of them. As the publication explains, the Oklahoma champion list, which is continually updated, has a broad appeal: "Many homeowners take great pride in having the largest specimen of a particular tree species in their yard. The Oklahoma champions are also submitted to the American Forestry Association to be recorded nationally. Oklahoma's champion black hickory is currently recognized as being the largest tree of its species in the entire United States!" According to *The Great Trees of Oklahoma*, this state- and national-champion black hickory measures 84 feet in height, with a circumference of 137 inches and a crown spread of 45 feet. The total point value for the tree—obtained by adding a tree's circumference in inches to its total height, in feet, to one-fourth (25 percent) its average crown spread, again in feet—is 232.

As impressive as this black hickory is, however, Oklahoma's champion pecan tree—interestingly, the pecan is also considered a hickory, as pecans are part of the genus *Carya,* which includes all hickories; pecans are the largest and fastest growing of the hickories—is larger and perhaps even more spectacular. *The Great Trees of Oklahoma* lists the pecan's height at 82 feet and its crown spread at 114 feet. But one of the things that make this tree so special is its circumference (its girth, or a measurement of the tree's trunk at a point four and one-half feet above the ground), which is 270 inches. That's twenty-two and one-half feet! Not surprisingly, Oklahoma's champion pecan tree has a total point value of 381, which makes it the state's fourth largest tree in terms of total points. Only the champion cottonwood, sycamore, and bald cypress are larger.

Which, at least for me, begs this question: how old is it? This is difficult to answer without taking a core sample. When I inquired with the US Fish & Wildlife Service, I was told its age is uncertain. They are confident that it's a native tree, however, and not a cultivated (grafted) specimen. Considering that the technique of grafting pecan trees wasn't widely embraced until around the turn of the twentieth century, this makes sense, because Oklahoma's champion pecan is likely much older than this.

A pecan scientist told me that this tree, being a native, can be "easily over 150 years old," adding that there have been native pecan trees in Oklahoma that are "several hundred years old."

While California's giant redwoods can live up to 2,000 years, and its giant sequoias longer still, living up to 3,000 years, and though the bristlecone pines of the American West can stand for 5,000 years, this does nothing to diminish pecans, in my opinion. After all, when you consider a tree that's endured a century or more of Oklahoma's volatile and often extreme weather, a tree that will outlive today's best and most carefully designed human dwellings and other structures while also providing some of nature's tastiest and most nutritious food, the resilience of native pecan trees is absolutely remarkable.

Indeed, its age is one of the most intriguing things about the Oklahoma champion pecan tree, as far as I'm concerned. As someone who has always believed he was born 70 or 100 years too late, and considering that time machines are products only of science fiction, I've had a lifelong fascination with windows into the past, especially when these decade- or century-leaping portals are not just dusty relics, but living, breathing witnesses to history.

Such is the case with Oklahoma's champion pecan, for if the assessment that the tree can be "easily over 150 years old" is correct, then this distinguished pecan sprouted from the ground around the time the American Civil War ended, or perhaps even decades before the 1861 firing on Fort Sumter, South Carolina, which triggered the war. This is fascinating, but it's not unusual. Native pecans often outlive even the world's oldest vertebrates, the giant tortoises of the Galápagos Islands, whose life spans average over 100 years and last as long as 152 years, according to *National Geographic*.

Given the tree's size, and considering the longevity of this species, it's easy to understand that the champion pecan was already a mature tree at the time Oklahoma became a state in 1907, that it photosynthesized the sun and carbon dioxide to produce oxygen that Teddy Roosevelt might have breathed, that it could have shaded my great-grandfather's family during their move from Texas into Indian Territory in 1889. If they traveled during late autumn, it's possible they may have gathered and eaten some of its pecans, or perhaps they used the tree as a landmark as they navigated their wagon and team of mules across the Red River and into history.

Though these settlers would constitute the first generation of European-descended residents in Indian Territory, the southern plains tribes had lived here for centuries, subsisting, at least in part, on pecans.

Some of these early Americans are believed to have traveled long distances specifically to harvest pecans, while other tribes settled in locations that were known to be in close proximity to expansive, highly productive groves. The Indians valued these nuts not only as a nutritious and easily obtainable food source but also as a commodity for trade between other tribes and, eventually, European travelers.

Fifteen minutes after hanging up with Joanne, a massive white pickup truck rumbled into the Tishomingo National Wildlife Refuge, rolling to a stop in front of my car. The passenger window went down, revealing a burly, bearded man, midthirties, with cap, sunglasses, and khaki shirt featuring a name patch: K Troxell. He introduced himself as Kyle, in a voice so soft, a demeanor so relaxed, that I wondered if he needed another cup of coffee.

"Climb in," he said. "We'll head over there."

So I opened the door and pulled myself up into the enormous vehicle, which I can best describe as a street-legal Abrams tank—one whose 120-mm cannon had been removed and replaced with US Fish & Wildlife Service decals on the doors. The pickup was mud crusted, inside and out. The interior resembled a mobile hardware/

Stands of naturally occurring (wild) pecan trees are called "groves." These trees, growing along a creek at the edge of an Oklahoma field, are located near a much larger grove of pecans that is continually being expanded with the aid of birds, such as blue jays and crows, and squirrels.

sporting-goods store. I spotted ropes, maps, binoculars, and a pair of camouflage chest waders among the inventory.

"How long have you been with the refuge?" I asked as we drove along the park's tree-lined road.

"Four and a half years," Kyle said. "I was in the air force for ten years before this. Did the same kind of work, running equipment, so it was a good fit."

"Thanks for keeping us safe," I said.

"I did three tours," he said, his sunglass-shaded eyes trained on the road ahead. "It sure is a lot better over here, I'll tell you that."

Glancing around at the refuge's quiet meadows and the greening forest, it wasn't hard to imagine why. As we headed toward the park's entrance, I asked Kyle about the champion pecan tree.

"You're the only one who's ever asked about it," he said. "I don't think many people know it's out here."

"Most people come here to fish, I guess."

"We have some of the best fishing right here in the refuge," he said. "I can't believe the size of fish they catch in Cumberland Pool, even from the shore. The state record blue catfish was caught there. Weighed like ninety-four pounds."

We exited the refuge and turned right at the high school, now heading east on a quiet two-lane highway.

If I had interrupted the day's work for Kyle, or his morning coffee, he didn't mention it. He was relaxed and polite, though reserved. He didn't speak much unless I asked a question. But when we passed a box turtle inching across the highway, his actions spoke volumes. He swerved to miss the turtle, then repeated the maneuver a few hundred yards later.

"It's that time of year," he said. "Turtles are on the move. A lot of people around here would have tried to hit them just then."

"That's terrible."

"I don't know why," he said. "They see a defenseless animal and they try to run it over."

After only a mile or two we turned off the highway into a verdant river bottom, wide open and immense. Distant trees hemmed the field's eastern and western edges, insulating it from the outside world like the hard shell of a nut. The river bottom was lush and teeming with birds and butterflies. The near side was covered in a dense, thigh-high jungle of planted rye and vetch. Kyle said each year the refuge plants the field in crops; harvesting is left to the wildlife.

In the distance was a lake of standing water.

We skirted the edge of the field in Kyle's truck until the tires began to slip.

"Uh-oh," he said, stopping the vehicle, reversing, and retreating onto solid ground. "We get stuck out here, it'll be hard to get out."

We climbed down from the pickup and walked the muddy trail, kicking through rye under a brilliant blue sky as we made for the standing water in the distance. "What's this up here?" I asked, pointing to some kind of cage in the trees off to our right.

"Hog trap," Kyle said. "That's a new model there, from the Noble Foundation. It works really good."

As we neared the cage, the stench of swine became palpable.

"We're overrun with wild hogs," he said. "They come out here and root around beneath these pecan trees. The native nuts are small, and they love them."

Just before we reached the water's edge, we passed a massive pecan tree, obviously a native. Its heavy, gnarled trunk, shaped by the elements over time, exuded a spirit of freedom and independence, and like a wily old boar it seemed to dominate the other, smaller specimens around it. This tree was unadulterated by humans. This tree was wild and free and unconquered. Judging by its considerable girth, it was easily over a hundred years old.

"That's an impressive tree," I said.

"The champion pecan is probably fifty percent larger than this one," Kyle said. "This is probably the second-biggest one out here, though."

As we continued our march, Kyle nodded toward the vast field to our left. "All this is grown up so thick because of the floods last year," he said. "You can see the trees we planted, those saplings there. Most of them didn't make it."

When we reached the water's edge, he motioned toward the river in the distance. "This water came up fast. There's a big log jam in the Washita River, and the water just backed up." Then he turned and pointed to the power lines at the edge of the road we'd driven in on. "See the bottom line?" he asked. "That's how high the water got in last year's floods."

It looked to be at least twenty feet off the ground. I couldn't imagine the water being so high, for only the tops of the surrounding trees would have been visible.

We continued our march, maneuvering along the waterline until Kyle stopped and pointed to some trees a half mile away, toward the western edge of the waterlogged field before us. "See that row of trees way out there?"

"That one?"

"Yeah," he said. "Now, do you see the one on the end, all the way to the left?"

"Got it."

"That's the champion pecan."

It was part of a small grove of giant pecan trees, an ancient's club of sorts. From this distance it looked no taller than the others around it, but I knew from the dimensions listed in *The Great Trees of Oklahoma* that its crown was considerable and its circumference even more impressive. Though I was relieved to have finally viewed it, I couldn't fully appreciate the tree from this distance. From where I stood, it resembled a clump of broccoli protruding from an immense plate of chicken broth. To fully grasp the tree's immense size, I knew I needed to see it up close. I was willing to wade out to the grove, but Kyle said the water was too deep. Besides, we'd already spotted a water moccasin back at the refuge, as well as several other snakes. This lake was undoubtedly hazardous to our health.

"It's under five or six feet of water," he said of the tree. "And there's deeper water between here and there."

As we made our way back to the pickup, my mind trying to work out how, exactly, I could get out to the tree, Kyle drew my attention to a large, decaying pecan that had fallen over the year before. "The soil was just too soft to hold it," he said. "We've had several of them collapse like that."

I hoped the champion pecan wouldn't be one of them.

—2—

Made in America

The pecan, *Carya illinoinensis*, evolved along the central and lower Mississippi River and its tributaries, from Illinois and Iowa in the north, south to the Gulf Coast and into Mexico, and from Texas east into Mississippi and, some believe, a portion of central Alabama. Wild pecans grow most prodigiously in the deep, well-drained alluvial soils of Arkansas, Louisiana, Oklahoma, and Texas, where the tree's long taproot extends to the water table while its system of lateral roots fans out to a spread twice or more than that of its branches. Its extensive and aggressive root system helped the pecan tree flourish in the riverine ecosystems where it evolved and where it still thrives today.

Pecans are actually something called a drupe, a type of fruit featuring a shell-encased seed, which is covered by a fleshy substance. With pecans, we eat the seed rather than the outer flesh. In a society that typically consumes a drupe's flesh while discarding the pit or the seed—think of a cherry or mango—this can be confusing. Fortunately, the US Department of Agriculture considers the pecan a nut. So does the *Merriam-Webster Dictionary*, and so do most of the growers and shellers I met and spoke to. After all, the crack and crunch we experience when shelling these and other nuts is altogether distinct from the way we access our fruits. Pecans differ greatly in size, ranging from tiny varieties such as the Cornfield and Martzahn, not much larger than acorns (along with many other wild, unnamed varieties, one of which I saw in Louisiana; it was smaller even than an acorn and similar in size to a standard, number-two pencil eraser) to the massive Podsednik and Doby, pecans resembling hen eggs. And like eggs, two or three of these nuts would probably make a good meal.

Pecans grow in clusters of several nuts, each encased in a thick hull that provides both nourishment and protection. In autumn the four-sided hulls split open and the ripened pecans fall to the ground. The shape of pecan nuts ranges from classically elliptical to oblong to almost perfectly round. Shell colors range from light tan to dark brown, and many are marked with black streaks. Meanwhile, kernel color varies from creamy tan to golden brown, according to the specific variety of pecan, and even these differ with respect to size, quality, and the portion of the overall nut they constitute.

The name "pecan" is a word of Algonquin origin referencing something approximating "a nut too hard to crack by hand" or "all nuts requiring a stone to crack." In any case, the nutritional value of the sweet kernel within was certainly worth the time and effort it took to extract it from the shell, especially for North America's earliest residents, many of whom grew to depend on the pecan as an import part of their diets. Along with its generous caloric value, pecans have an appealing flavor and they could be stored for a time, which allowed the Indians to consume these nuts weeks or months after they had been gathered and throughout the winter. These qualities helped make pecans a dietary staple in many early American Indian cultures.

When Europeans were introduced to the pecan, they tended to view it as a type of walnut—a nut they were familiar with from the Old World and which they often brought with them and planted in their travels in North America.

Spanish explorer Álvar Núñez Cabeza de Vaca wrote about these "walnuts" in his diary. After being shipwrecked on a sandy island off the coast of present-day Texas in 1528, Cabeza de Vaca eventually traveled to what is thought to be the Guadalupe River, where he noted these nuts grew in such abundance that the natives ate nothing else for two months of the year.

George Washington is said to have enjoyed snacking on pecans, and he experimented with plantings of dozens of different crops, including pecans, at Mount Vernon. For Thomas Jefferson, pecans were a source of fascination. He once wrote home from Paris asking for a shipment of these American nuts, and as his garden book indicates, he planted hundreds of pecans on his Monticello estate. This included a 1794 planting of 200 pecans, and in 1802 a follow-up planting of what he called a "great number" of the nuts. Jefferson's January 16, 1800, letter to Daniel Clark mentions two twenty-year-old pecan trees that had not yet produced fruit. Yet, despite this, his success in growing the trees in Virginia, well outside their native range, seems to have prompted him to mention that they could be raised there and that he was determined to have a grove of them. After receiving a shipment of these nuts from William Charles Cole Claiborne, Jefferson wrote in an 1806 letter that he was always receptive to receiving pecans, which he found favorable both for planting and table use.

Pecans helped nourish the first Texas army in its battle for independence from Mexico. In his book *The Evolution of a State* (1900), Noah Smithwick highlights a scene from the 1835 Battle of Concepción in which rebel forces, taking cover during a volley of Mexican cannon fire, lay low while shot crashed through the pecan trees overhead, showering the men with nuts. The author then describes some of the rebels picking up these fallen pecans and casually eating them as if they'd been dislodged by the wind.

Thomas F. De Voe included a listing for pecans in his 1867 compendium, *The Market Assistant,* which claimed to include a brief description of every article of human food sold in the public markets of New York, Boston, Philadelphia, and Brooklyn. Describing the pecan, he wrote, "These nuts are brought from the South and West, and are taken for a species of the *Hickory Nut,* known by some as the *Illinois Hickory.* It is almost an inch long, as large as the end of a common-sized finger, with a smooth shell, and oblong shape. They are of an agreeable taste and wholesome. Brought here principally from the Southern States and Texas, and in season from December until April."

In his 1905 treatise on the pawpaw, James Little writes of a particularly severe drought in the year 1860, which parched the landscape of the southern Kansas Territory. Little notes that it was the worst drought ever known in Kansas and that it would last for eighteen months. The Neosho River went dry. No farm products were produced. Settlers were in a "starving condition," and a good many were leaving the country. Mercifully, this was also a time of one of the heaviest nut crops ever known in the Neosho bottoms. According to Little, settlers spent a great deal of time in the woods with their hammers, cracking open the pecans that helped them survive.

When the Cherokee, Choctaw, Chickasaw, Creek, and Seminole arrived in present-day Oklahoma in the 1830s, they began clearing river bottoms for crops, typically leaving the groves of native pecan trees they encountered. They valued this wild crop both for food and trading. Pecans were so important that many Indian tribes enacted laws to protect the trees. An 1876 Chickasaw Nation law, for example, prohibited the destruction of pecan trees and even the cutting of a single limb for purposes of gathering nuts. Fines for doing so ranged from $25–$50. Similarly, Section 152 of the Muskogee Nation's 1892 constitution specified that anyone cutting down any pecan tree, for the purpose of obtaining the fruit thereof, would be fined $25 per tree destroyed. The law further stipulated that $10 of the fine would be paid to the informant and the remainder remitted to the Muskogee national treasury.

Considering their North American origin, it's no surprise that pecans should figure into the myths and folktales of some of our continent's earliest human inhabitants. The Caddo peoples traditionally lived in an area roughly encompassing what is today southwest Arkansas, northwest Louisiana, southeast Oklahoma, and northeast Texas. Although their language is related to that of many plains tribes, Caddo culture was more closely associated with some of the southeastern tribes, including the Choctaw, Chickasaw, and Natchez. The Caddo were agriculturalists who raised corn, beans, squash, and other crops. They supplemented their diets by hunting and fishing and by gathering the wild fruits and nuts available to them, such as the pecan, which abounded in these fertile river-bottom landscapes.

One of the Caddo's many folktales was a story referred to as "The Old Woman Who Kept All the Pecans," which Caddo storytellers in Oklahoma relayed to researcher George Dorsey early in the twentieth century:

> There lived an old woman who was mother to all the pecan trees. She owned all of the trees and gathered all of the nuts herself. When people went to her lodge she would give them a few pecans to eat, but would never allow them to take any away. The people were very fond of pecans and they wanted some for their own use, but the old woman would not let them have any. One time the people were very hungry and the old woman had everything in her lodge filled with pecans, but she would give them only a few when they went to see her and she made them eat them before going away. This made the people angry and they decided that something must be done.
>
> There was in the village an old man who had four little sons who were very troublesome and meddlesome. The people—they were the field Rats—thought that these four little boys would be the right ones to go over to the old woman's house some night to try to steal some of the nuts. They chose the four boys both because they were small

> and quiet and sly and because they were such a nuisance around the village that they would be no great loss to the people if the old woman killed them. The Rats were willing to go because they were always glad to be meddling. They chose one to slip over and make sure that the old woman was asleep. He went to her lodge and peeped in through a small crack and saw that she was still at work. He waited until she finished her work and went to bed; then when he heard her snore he ran back home to tell his brothers to come. When he went outside his father's lodge he saw a stranger sitting there. The stranger was Coyote. He had come to tell the Rats not to trouble about stealing pecans from the old woman, for he was going over the next day and kill her. Coyote was afraid to trust the Rats. He wanted to go himself, so he could get the most of the pecans. The next morning he went over to see the old woman and acted very friendly. The old woman gave him some pecans and he sat down and ate them all up. Then he asked her for some more, and as she turned around to get them he pulled out his stone knife and struck her on the head. She died, and ever since then the pecan trees have grown everywhere and belong to all of the people.

This folktale is significant not only because it highlights pecans as an important food item for the early Caddo, as well as something central to their culture, but also for its almost inevitable inclusion of the coyote—or in this case, *Coyote,* that ancient trickster possessing a full range of human traits. Like the pecan, the coyote is an American original, having emerged from a line of ancestral canids that evolved in the American Southwest. And like the pecan tree, which has broadened its range over the past century, albeit with human assistance, coyotes, also with our help—and amid, and in spite of, our presence—have expanded their native range to the point that, like the pecan, today they're found across the United States, from the Atlantic to the Pacific.

America's pecan crop traditionally came from native and seedling trees. Yet the industry is based on the science of grafting. Because pecans do not come true to seed, which is to say that pecan seeds do not produce trees with qualities identical to those of the parent stock, grafting is vital for commercial pecan production. This is the only way to produce pecans of consistent quality and character. There is an old story pecan growers often tell about the farmer who found a pecan tree he liked and decided to plant an orchard. He collected five hundred pecans from this tree and planted them, thinking he would get five hundred clones. Later, as the trees matured and began producing, he was shocked to realize that what was growing in his orchard were five hundred different pecan-tree varieties.

While this tendency toward inconsistency was a challenge to be overcome for commercial production, the pecan's proclivity for genetic diversification is a survival mechanism developed over thousands of years of evolution. Most pecan trees are incapable of self-pollination. Although they're monoecious, with each tree developing both pistil and stamen flowers, these flowers mature at different times. Some varieties exhibit protogynous behavior, in which a tree's female flowers (pistils) are receptive to fertilization before its pollen is released. In protandrous varieties, on the other hand, male flowers (catkins) come into bloom and shed clouds of pollen before the female flowers mature. Pecan growers refer to these two different varieties as Type I and Type II trees. Successful orchards or groves (blocks of trees planted by humans are referred to as "orchards," while stands of naturally occurring—wild—pecan trees are called "groves") require both types.

Pecan trees are wind pollinated. In nature pollen from a protandrous tree may fertilize a protogynous variety in a neighboring field. In commercial orchards growers plant at least two (and often several) varieties to ensure fertilization, and they plant them in close proximity to one another. Thus, growers must know which tree varieties they

The pecan stands alone, both for its inimitable flavor and its status as North America's only indigenous tree nut to have been developed into a significant, enduring, and highly successful commercial agricultural crop.

own and which varieties are compatible. A Kansas pecan man told me that for new orchards he prefers to graft in four different cultivars in order to minimize the risk of crop failure. He said this could be a half/half combination of flowering types, or even a one-fourth ratio, so long as a pollinator is planted no more than four rows away from any one cultivar.

As is often pointed out, pecans are the only major tree nuts indigenous to North America. What is less frequently mentioned, though perhaps more revealing, is that pecans are our only commercialized crop of native tree nuts, and among the few native North American plant species of any type to be developed into a significant agricultural industry. And while pecans produced from native and seedling trees continue to figure into the annual US harvest, the industry has proliferated on the advent of improved varieties.

States such as Kansas, Missouri, Louisiana, Oklahoma, Arkansas, Mississippi, and Texas have always had groves of wild pecan trees, but it wasn't until farmers and nursery owners embraced the process of grafting in earnest just after the turn of the twentieth century that the pecan industry began to grow exponentially. Only a few years earlier, grafted pecan trees were still relatively uncommon. In his 1896 book, *The Nut Culturist: A Treatise on the Propagation, Planting, and Cultivation of Nut-Bearing Trees and Shrubs Adapted to the Climate of the United States*, New Jersey writer and editor Andrew S. Fuller laments the difficulty he experienced in acquiring these trees at the time. "Having been repeatedly assured, by men who presumed to know," he writes, "that the pecan tree was successfully propagated in the South by grafting, and many thousands annually raised in this way, it seems strange that such plants are so rarely offered by nurserymen."

Fuller's interest in pecans stemmed from his background in horticulture and botany and also a belief in enhancing America's inventory of nut-producing trees as a means for a growing nation to more easily feed itself. Describing his vision for *The Nut Culturist*, he explains in the book's preface, "I have not advised the general planting of nut orchards on land adapted to the production of grain and other indispensable farm crops, but mainly as roadside trees, and where desired for shade, shelter and ornament, being confident that when all such positions are occupied with choice nut-bearing trees, to the exclusion of those yielding nothing of intrinsic value, there will have been added many millions of dollars to the wealth of the country, as well as a vast store of edible and delicious food."

Realizing that southern varieties would struggle in the northern climate, Fuller appealed to his readers to seek those "thoroughly acclimated trees" from the pecan's northern limits, places like Missouri, Illinois, and Iowa, which he believed would allow for the extension of their cultivation well north of the tree's natural range. Indeed, the grounds of his own New Jersey home featured "some fifty or more" pecan trees that he'd grown from seeds sent by a Judge Samuel Miller of Bluffton, Missouri. At the time he wrote *The Nut Culturist,* all these trees had proven hearty enough to withstand his northern winters. But Fuller envisioned even greater possibilities for pecan trees produced through grafting, recognizing the process as "probably the most practical means of multiplying them, and at the same time preserving their varietal characteristics."

Eventually he appealed to P. J. Berckmans of the Fruitland Nurseries of Augusta, Georgia, whose "experience and acquaintance with the fruits of the South" were, Fuller wrote, "without doubt, in advance of any other horticulturalist of the past or even the present generation." Though the Stuart Pecan Company had recently published *The Pecan and How to Grow It* (1893), which included a section on grafting, with instructions for performing such techniques as "annular budding," "tongue graft," and the "cleft graft," Berckmans's reply offers some indication of the difficulties associated with this method of propagation at the time:

> For the past five or six years we have grafted various varieties of the pecan nuts. I do not know of any other nurseryman South who offers grafted trees. I presume the reason of this is, the great difficulty in having the grafts take, as we seldom have more than fifteen to twenty-five percent grow. We usually crown graft in February, using one-year-old seedlings grown in nursery rows. Owing to the small percentage of grafts which grow, grafted trees must, necessarily, be quite expensive, and for this reason there are so few attempts made in this method of propagation.

The Pecan and How to Grow It, which was informed by Colonel W. R. Stuart's research in pecan grafting and the development of improved varieties during the late 1880s and early 1890s, echoed these challenges. Stuart writes that grafting pecans was more difficult than with other trees and that only a very small percentage of such grafts was successful. For this reason, and the fact that the grafting of pecan trees was still a developing practice in the 1890s, the supply of desirable graft wood—that producing what Stuart called "a first-class nut"—with which to work was extremely limited, thereby slowing grafting's progress through the pecan belt. This would soon change, however, as Col. Stuart's research gradually helped transform the industry.

In the early 1900s agricultural scientists and extension agents urged farmers to abandon seedlings and focus their efforts instead on grafting. This was the future of the industry, and related messaging began to reflect this. An early prospectus for the New Orleans Pecan Nursery Company, for example, contained an advertisement encouraging the planting of not just pecans, but grafted, papershell pecan trees, a message augmented significantly by the image of a basket brimming with large, well-formed pecans of a very consistent size and character. This message was further supported by several of the publication's articles, including "It Pays to Plant Grafted Pecan Trees," and "Pecan Seedlings Versus Grafted or Budded Trees." The latter piece explained that planting pecan trees from seed required a wait of ten to fifteen years and would invariably result in a number of "worthless trees on hand of which not two are alike," while adding that grafted trees will bear in only a few years. Given this, "it would be folly to attempt growing from seed," the article noted. Similarly, in his 1910 book, *The Pecan and Its Culture,* author H. Harold Hume explained that for most farmers, the greatest objection to grafted trees was the cost. And yet, despite this, Hume wrote that it was better to plant grafted trees, even if fewer of them were planted.

Historian James McWilliams reports in *The Pecan: A History of America's Native Nut* that between 1900 and 1925 Alabama's orchard tree count grew from 25,000 to 170,000. The growth of South Carolina's orchards was even more dramatic, increasing from 10,000 to

200,000 trees, while the number of cultivated trees in Mississippi went from 40,000 to 710,000. Most impressive of all was Georgia, which increased its inventory of 30,000 trees to nearly 2.4 million. McWilliams writes that during these crucial years the pecan industry reached a "tipping point" as grafting gradually became an accepted and mainstream form of cultivation, allowing growers to essentially manufacture trees rather than planting them from seed. And while landowners had been raising pecans for decades through the planting of seedlings and through the selective thinning of naturally occurring stands of trees, as the aforementioned numbers indicate, the difference brought about through grafting was so significant that it seemed an altogether new and different American industry had been created. The pecan's value and reputation soared.

In her 1994 book, *The Pecan Tree,* Jane Manaster describes an emotional outburst by one E. W. Kirkpatrick—an associate of the late Texas governor Jim Hogg, whose deathbed request to have a pecan tree planted at his grave led to the state's adoption in 1919 of the pecan as its state tree—at a 1907 assembly of the Texas Nut Growers' Association. "We have pursued the wrong course in neglecting the pecan," Kirkpatrick stated, calling it a more profitable thing than the walnut groves of California. "It excels," he said, "the olive, orange, the lemon, the peach, the apricot, the prune, and the grape: it excels everything."

As the aforementioned tree numbers suggest, it would seem that by this point the burgeoning pecan industry was beginning to believe him.

As pecan farming expanded so too did pecan shelling, particularly in San Antonio, Texas. For many years the Lone Star State produced roughly half the nation's total seedling crop, much of which was grown within a 250-mile radius of the city. The close proximity of such a large proportion of the commercial pecan crop, along with an abundant source of cheap labor, helped make San Antonio a major center for pecan shelling. As noted in *The Pecan Shellers of San Antonio,* a

1940 report produced by the US Work Projects Administration, the city reached a peak of more than 400 shelling establishments, employing up to 20,000 workers, mostly Latinos, during 1933–1934. Pecan shelling was a major source of employment for Mexican Americans in San Antonio during the Great Depression, despite being one of the lowest-paid industries in the nation. Richard Garcia writes in *Rise of the Mexican American Middle Class* that pecan shelling thrived during the 1930s because it required only workers and space. Although the shelling companies made large profits, they paid very low wages. Equally as problematic were the working conditions, which were by all accounts abysmal. Shellers crowded around tables in dimly illuminated, poorly ventilated rooms that often lacked toilets and wash facilities. A fine dust, the residue of the cracked pecan shells, permeated the air in these workrooms. Many maintained that this dust contributed to various respiratory ailments, including a disproportionate rate of tuberculosis among the city's Mexican American community.

Prior to the Depression the shelling industry was largely mechanized. The nuts were cracked and graded by machine, though the removal of pecan meats from shells was still performed by hand, even in 1928, when the San Antonio shelling industry reached its peak of mechanization. During the Great Depression the shelling companies realized they could save money by reversing the trend toward machines, and hand labor was reinstituted.

On January 31, 1938, approximately 12,000 San Antonio pecan shellers, mostly women, walked off their jobs to protest a wage cut that reduced their earnings from six cents per pound for pieces, and seven cents a pound for halves, to five and six cents per pound, respectively. The workers were organized under the International Pecan Shellers Union #172 and led initially by the outspoken and controversial Emma Tenayuca, a well-known San Antonio labor organizer and activist. City police responded with force, deploying riot squads to break up picket lines and arresting hundreds, including Tenayuca, whose fiery speeches helped attract national attention to the strike. When both sides agreed to arbitration five weeks later, the shellers returned to work awaiting the arbitration board's decision. The result was a wage increase for the pecan shellers.

Success was fleeting, however. In October 1938 the Fair Labor Relations Act went into effect, mandating a minimum wage of twenty-five cents per hour. Although this was intended to establish a fair wage and improve living conditions for workers, it had the opposite effect for the pecan shellers of San Antonio. Gradually, mechanization was reinstituted. Those who were able to retain their jobs now earned double or sometimes triple their former wages, yet cracking machines were rapidly eliminating the need for workers. By 1941, 10,000 pecan shellers had lost their jobs to mechanization, and by the end of the decade Pecan Shellers Union #172, which had represented the workers in their strike ten years earlier, had dissolved.

Despite this, the 1938 San Antonio pecan shellers' strike is considered a success. Through the help of national labor leaders and close organization, the pecan shellers were able to challenge the city's industrial power brokers and force the industry operators to the bargaining table. Many historians consider this the first significant labor victory for Mexican American workers in US history.

Cities and towns across the United States feature streets named after all sorts of things, especially trees. As you might expect, pecans figure prominently into the infrastructure of many of these communities, especially in the South. Oklahoma City, for example, has a Pecan Lane. Noble, the tiny central-Oklahoma community where my great-grandfather spent most of his 102 years on this earth, has a Pecan Street, where many of the houses used to be, and probably still are, shaded by pecan trees. And Norman, my hometown, has a Pecan Avenue.

Across the American South, particularly in Texas, where the pecan is the state tree, one can find everything from residential apartments, schools, and neighborhood subdivisions, to restaurants, farms and ranches, churches, outdoor markets, dry cleaners, laundries, car washes, breweries, shopping malls, medical and dental facilities, office parks, and various athletic clubs, all named for the ubiquitous pecan.

In his book *A Journal of Travels into the Arkansas Territory, during the Year 1819* (1821), Thomas Nuttall wrote of a settlement called the Pecannerie situated along the Arkansas River, so named for the forest of pecan trees surrounding it. Today Arkansas is home to Pecan Point, a tiny community along the Mississippi River, a name it shares with the Pecan Point Brewing Company of Texarkana, Texas, and also an area along the nearby Red River where, in 1818, Rev. William Stevenson, a Methodist preacher, held the first Protestant church service in what is today the great state of Oklahoma. There's even a Pecan Grove, Texas, a small community near Houston, named for the area's pecan trees and featuring such amenities as a Pecan Grove Park and Pecan Lakes.

In southern Louisiana near the Gulf of Mexico, in Vermilion Parish, is a community situated on shallow ridges of shell and sand deposits known as *cheniers*. The ridges are slightly elevated above the surrounding coastal marsh, and they traditionally supported a number of trees, particularly live oaks. Although its foundation lies in these cheniers—a French term for *place of oaks*—the community is named Pecan Island.

Glenwood, an autism and behavioral health center in Birmingham, Alabama, holds a Pecans for Autism program each fall with proceeds helping fund essential Glenwood programs and services for children, adolescents, adults, and families. Glenwood sources its pecans from growers in Alabama, Mississippi, Georgia, and Florida and offers a variety of products ranging from mammoth halves to pecans coated in cinnamon, chocolate, Cajun spice, and honey, as well as pecan-popcorn mixes and even fried pecans, a new product featuring

The Garden Club of Jacksonville, Florida, sells pecans each autumn as part of an annual fundraising event. Signs like this one are common throughout the American South during the fall months and are today being seen in areas outside this tree nut's traditional range, such as New Mexico and Arizona, where pecans have become a cultural, and economic, staple.

kernels coated in sugar and salt, then flash fried. The facility ships pecans across Alabama and beyond and offers them through local businesses and grocery stores. What began as a holiday pecan sale nearly forty years ago has grown into a program with over $600,000 in revenues each year because, as staff and volunteers like to say, Glenwood's pecans have a purpose.

Whether you pronounce pecan, "puh-KHAN," with the emphasis on the second syllable, as they do in Oklahoma and Texas, or "PE-can," emphasizing the first syllable as they do in Georgia, or as some kind of hybrid of the two, such as "PE-khan," as I've so often heard in California, this nut's value as a food item extends far beyond what is perhaps its most famous product, pecan pie.

Not long ago, while traveling through South Carolina, I stopped at a roadside cider stand. It was hot. I was thirsty. A cold glass of cider sounded wonderful. Once I stepped inside and looked around, however, I realized the sign outside should have read "PECANS" instead of "FRESH CIDER." That's because I found much more of the former than the latter. There were pecans still in the shell and roasted pecans that had already been shelled. There were also candied pecans, spicy pecans, pecan logs, pecan flour, pecan oil, and probably many other pecan-based products. I settled for a pecan praline and a bottle of water. At the cash register I asked the clerk where her store's pecans came from. She laughed and said "PE-cans" grow everywhere.

Though traditionally associated with the South and with the Thanksgiving and Christmas holidays, today pecans are eaten in many countries around the world, including Australia, South Africa, Israel, and China, to name a few. Here at home they're used in all sorts of products and especially as ingredients in many of our favorite snacks, such as butter-pecan ice cream. According to Dan Zedan of Nature's Finest Foods, an Illinois-based organization specializing in the marketing of tree nuts, butter pecan is the third, fourth, or fifth best-selling flavor of every major ice cream company in North America as of 2016. Then there is something called the "pecan turtle," which consists of a cluster of these nuts drizzled first in caramel and then in either milk chocolate or dark chocolate. Zedan says it's one of the best-selling confection items in the United States.

The Georgia Pecan Commission, an organization working to increase demand for its namesake nut, offers a multitude of pecan-rich recipes. These include dishes such as sautéed scallops with lemon, parsley, and Georgia pecans; vegetable and Georgia pecan calzones; and spiced snapper with Georgia pecan crust, among many others.

Aside from a truly remarkable job of branding its state's pecans, the commission's dozens of recipes suggest—and there's no reason to believe otherwise—that these nuts are as versatile as they are nutritious and tasty. If you're skeptical, then consider that pecans are used in the creation of such foods as butter, bread, oil, crackers, cheese, cakes, protein bars, various dips, sundry dressings, pancake and waffle mixes, and beverages such as pecan-flavored tea, and even pecan milk, a non-dairy, vegan alternative to cow's milk. Lafcadio Hearn's *Creole Cook Book,* published in 1885 and said to be the first Creole cookbook ever written, includes a simple and appetizing recipe for pecan cake.

Long a fan of peanut brittle, just the other day I had the opportunity to sample a similar candy made with pecans. It was much darker in color than peanut brittle, with a more distinctive flavor, thanks in part to the heavy corn syrup used to create it. The storekeeper who insisted I try the pecan brittle tells me she sells enough of this highly addictive indulgence to pay for her daughter's college tuition. This experience came just hours after visiting with the judges of a cooking contest whose winning entry was a cookie made with pecan flour. Evidently, the baker—a "little old lady," as the judges referred to her—had used pecan flour because she wanted her cookies to be gluten-free. But it was the flavor this flour (which is often referred to as pecan meal) imparted to the cookies that powered them to victory over the second-place dish—a sweet potato and pecan cheesecake made by a professional chef.

Recently, while visiting northern Michigan where I enjoyed, among other foods, a delicious dish known as pecan-crusted whitefish, I spotted something curious in the grocery store cooler. For some reason, though the cooler was filled with dozens of different beverages, an assortment of bottles and labels, my eyes locked onto one specific product. Squinting, thinking my eyes were deceiving me, I moved closer for a better view. I've been told by more than one industry insider that pecans aren't always available in all parts of the United States, that certain places, such as here in the North, don't always have them (perhaps because in the North, walnuts or almonds, say, might have more top-of-mind awareness thanks in part to a lack of pecan-industry marketing, and partly to pecans having long been something of a niche industry when compared to these giants). But I was pleasantly surprised to see there in the grocery store cooler a bottle of cold-brewed pecan-flavored coffee. And I wondered: who buys this? The answer: no one I noticed in the few minutes I loitered around the cooler. Before moving on I checked the bottle to see where this coffee was produced. The answer: Austin, Texas.

And then there's beer.

The Seguin Brewing Company of Seguin, Texas, offers a Honey Pecan #5, which it describes as its flagship beer, well balanced and "not too sweet and not too nutty." Until recently, the Abita Brewing Company in Louisiana offered a Bourbon Street Maple Pecan beer, described as a bourbon, barrel-aged, nut-brown ale. A company representative told me the Bourbon Street Maple Pecan did not make the cut for the company's 2018 production plans, although she added that these brews can make a comeback at any time. Not far away, in the great state of Mississippi, the Lazy Magnolia Brewing Company offers its Southern Pecan Nut Brown Ale. The company claims it is the first beer in the world to its knowledge made with whole roasted pecans. This brew won a bronze medal for specialty beers at the 2006 World Beer Cup.

While other types of nuts might have been chosen as ingredients for these beverages, the brewers selected pecans at least partly—or primarily, one imagines—for their flavor. After all, pecans aren't the least expensive nuts around. And since its many health benefits seem irrelevant when considering an ingredient for brewing beer, flavor begins to emerge as the chief (or perhaps sole) criterion.

Taste preferences are very subjective, Zedan told me in a June 2016 interview. They vary by person and by region. In California most would prefer walnuts, almonds, or pistachios. But in the South, it's pecans.

As is evidenced by my wonderful discovery in Michigan, however, this may be changing as more people outside the traditional South are introduced to America's indigenous tree nut. A case in point: a recent study on pecan oil at New Mexico State University in which consumers compared the flavor of breads soaked in olive and pecan oils before sampling salad dressings made from the two oils. The results are fascinating. Of the forty-one people participating in the study, some thirty-one stated a preference for the pecan oil. Then, after learning about the health benefits of pecan oil—among others, low in saturated fats and high in heart-healthy unsaturated fatty acids—eight of the ten who had chosen the olive oil changed their minds and stated a preference for pecan oil.

Perhaps the study's participants were biased given their location in New Mexico, currently the nation's second-largest producer of this crop. Or maybe they just like the pecan's flavor. In any case, pecan-oil processors must be encouraged by these results considering that their product fared so well against olive oil, which would seem to be the standard by which all other cooking oils are judged.

Despite its inimitable flavor and versatility in the kitchen, despite being so closely associated with our Thanksgiving and Christmas holidays, and though it's the basis for one of our nation's most popular and quintessential desserts, the pecan has managed to transcend the culinary world and has come to symbolize America itself. This is particularly true in places such as China, where demand for pecans is growing exponentially. A growing Chinese middle class means more discretionary income and a giant Asian nation clamoring for all things American, such as the pecan, a delectable and supremely healthful food that not only originated in North America, but also one that the United States produces better than anyone else. It's a portable terroir, an in-shell accumulation of sunlight, air, water, and American soil, an edible amalgam of our nation's inheritance, ingenuity, and potential. But considering this nut's history and the botanical niche it constitutes, this seems only fitting. After all, pecans originated here. For thousands of years they were a dietary staple of many American Indian tribes. They were a favorite snack for some of our nation's founders. Like the populace they represent, pecans are genetically diverse, and this diversity benefits the trees and the ecosystems in which they're found. They've been with us throughout our nation's history; they've persisted, and have even expanded their presence over the years. Of the myriad commodities we can offer the world, what's more American than our pecans?

As a cultural icon, the pecan's influence extends beyond our kitchens and into the art world, where pecan-inspired paintings, drawings, photographs, and literary references immerse us in the essence of place, America, and especially the American South, while symbolizing the concept of Americana. Eudora Welty, in an October 1943 letter to her beau, John Robinson, who was away at war, commented that the pecans in her Jackson, Mississippi, neighborhood were still a bit green. Nevertheless, perhaps as a symbol of the couple's budding romance, or simply as a tangible reminder of home, Welty picked a few of these pecans and sent them to Robinson along with some book reviews.

In *Blue Highways* (1982), author William Least Heat-Moon describes traveling along Mississippi's Natchez Trace and passing "pastures and pecan groves and tilled fields." At a Baptist college he meets a woman whose freshly curled hair was "dropped in loose coils the color of polished pecan."

Decca Records released in 1955 a David Holt and Robert Wells song, "Mississippi Pecan Pie" (Decca 29538), recorded by American singer and actor Gary Crosby, eldest son of the legendary performer, Bing Crosby. Music-industry magazine, the *Cash Box*, reviewed this number for its May 28, 1955, issue, giving it a rating of "C+" which equated to "good," and citing "Mississippi Pecan Pie" as "another cute novelty."

One of the most bizarre references comes to us from that master of the macabre, Lafcadio Hearn, whose *Historical Sketch Book and Guide to New Orleans and Environs* (1885) includes a story about the last public execution in New Orleans, a tale later collected in S. Frederick Starr's *Inventing New Orleans* (2001). According to Hearn, two condemned men stood on the gallows awaiting their fate while a crowd of witnesses gathered around them. The weather that day was dark and gloomy, and "angry flashes of lightning" illuminated the scene with "short lurid darts of flame." At the moment the trap fell, a bolt of lightning flashed, followed by a burst of thunder. Torrents of rain began falling, scattering the terrified crowd. When they managed to regain their composure and look again at the gallows, "ropes were seen dangling and swaying loosely in the wind, for there was nothing at the lower end." Beneath the gallows, two forms were seen lying on the pavement, one writhing in pain, and the other trying to crawl away from his fate. Hearn writes that the crowd began to commiserate with these two unfortunate souls, and at this point the public sentiment turned in their favor, heralding an inevitable riot. Yet, "the law was inexorable," Hearn notes, "and its servants were compelled to perform their horrible duty." Amid the pouring rain, the two convicts were picked up and conducted back to the gallows where they were hanged, much to the disgust of the now-furious crowd. Even with a force of two hundred men, the police struggled to contain the mob. According to Hearn, the crowd was so outraged that at its next session the Louisiana legislature was compelled to pass a law prohibiting public executions.

The crime that heralded this grisly event? It seems these two men, one a Creole, the other a Frenchman, had murdered a woman whom they'd witnessed secreting what they thought was a coin or another object of some value. Imagine their consternation, their utter befuddlement, when, after their heinous deed, they uncovered not silver nor gold, but a bag of pecans.

Far less dramatic was the Georgia pecan grower I visited who had a framed sketch of a pecan-nut cluster displayed on his office wall, a microcosm of the thousand-acre orchard surrounding his office, where nascent pecan clusters were just beginning to develop. Later, while admiring what I considered the company's most artistically significant product, its pecan pie, which was blanketed in a brown quilt of mammoth-sized kernels, the framed sketch on the wall began to make perfect sense. For while the office and building were constructed of wood and concrete, these same pecan clusters—and the hundreds of thousands of them occurring each year throughout the surrounding orchards—formed the basis for the entire operation, including this man's livelihood and that of his staff.

The Alluvian, a boutique hotel in Greenwood, Mississippi, features in its lobby a painting entitled "Millsaps Pecan Grove at Dusk" by the artist Collier Parker. Parker, formerly dean of the College of Arts and Sciences at Delta State University in nearby Cleveland, Mississippi, is today a professor of art at the Insalaco College of Creative and Performing Arts at Marywood University in Scranton, Pennsylvania. He told me he created this piece from a smaller, original painting he made on-site in the pecan grove one evening in an attempt to replicate the light and color of the setting Delta sun. The painting is certainly remarkable for its evocation of this light, and it manages to capture the majesty of these vine-encased old-growth pecan trees at that magic moment when the horizon begins to absorb the sun and the ambient light warms and softens and bathes the landscape in evening's easy embrace. In viewing the painting one feels a part of the pecan grove, and from this perspective the combination of shade and filtered light becomes almost palpable. There is a certain anonymity, a safety even, in viewing the distant field from the haven afforded by these majestic old trees. And in the far distance we see the horizon, aglow in evening's slow farewell, a sight we share with our arboreal neighbors. Through these qualities, "Millsaps Pecan Grove at Dusk" evokes a strong sense of place, perfect for a boutique hotel whose décor reflects the colors and mystique of the surrounding alluvial-plain landscape.

Clementine Hunter was one of the twentieth century's most celebrated Southern artists. She was born on Hidden Hill Plantation in the Cane River country of north-central Louisiana in December of 1886 or January of 1887. She would live to be 101, never venturing far from her birthplace and working for much of her life on Melrose Plantation in Natchitoches Parish. Under the guidance of its owner, Cammie Henry, Melrose Plantation became an artist's retreat, hosting painters and writers who stayed on the plantation while they worked. One day Hunter found some tubes of paint left behind by one of these artist guests, and she set about creating her very first painting on a discarded window shade. Hunter would eventually produce over 5,000 paintings on a variety of materials ranging from canvas and wood to jugs, bottles, and many others. She was a self-taught folk artist who worked from memory, producing images of early twentieth-century plantation life, a bygone era she had known and lived through. Her paintings depict scenes of washing clothes, picking cotton, fishing, baptisms, weddings, and funerals. Hunter was already in her fifties when she began painting, and these early works she often gave away to friends or sold for as little as a quarter. Today her work fetches thousands of dollars and is included in the collections of the Dallas Museum of Fine Art, the Smithsonian American Art Museum, the American Folk Art Museum, Minneapolis Institute of Arts, and other institutions.

One of my favorite Clementine Hunter works is a painting referred to simply as "Pecan Threshing." It features a plantation worker using a long pole to shake pecans from trees as the nuts shower the ground. Other workers are gathering the pecans and placing them into baskets. During autumn, Hunter is said to have worked six days a week picking pecans, a crop that grew in abundance on Melrose

Plantation and that today remains a staple of Louisiana's Cane River region. These vast orchards along with Hunter's memories of gathering pecans were so indelibly imprinted on her mind that she included images of the pecan harvest in her famous African House murals, her most ambitious and acclaimed work as an artist.

Clementine Hunter has been celebrated over the years not only as an artist but also as an important social and cultural historian. The scenes of plantation life depicted in "Pecan Threshing" and her African House murals, with their significant historical details, are major reasons for that acclaim.

Today, the Courthouse-on-the-Square Museum in Denton, Texas, claims to have the world's largest collection of pecan art. According to Kelsey Jistel, museum services coordinator, this inventory includes 300 pieces created by one B. W. Crawford, a man once known as the Pecan Picasso. Crawford used whole pecans—one of our culture's truest and most organic icons—to create whimsical representations of other American icons, such as Elvis Presley and George Washington. One of his most popular works is based on C. M. Coolidge's famous paintings of poker-playing dogs.

Jistel told me the facility displays only a few pieces of Crawford's pecan art on any given day. At the time of my inquiry in 2016, this included artistic representations of Snow White and the Seven Dwarfs, Marilyn Monroe, Elvis Presley, and Dolly Parton. Approximately 100 pieces of Crawford's work were then on loan to the Pecan Museum of Texas, in Seguin, a new facility with the mission of promoting the pecan industry and honoring its contributors, past and present. Part of the Texas Agriculture Education and Heritage Center, the museum is a featured attraction in Seguin's annual Pecan Fest Heritage Days—described as a three-day celebration of all things pecan and all things Seguin—along with a pecan bake-off, pecan queen contest, and Pecan Fest pub crawl, among other events. This is a lot of pecans, but for a city often referred to as the "pecan capital" of Texas, or perhaps more

Pape Pecan Company's Nutcracker Museum in Seguin, Texas.

accurately as a big pecan orchard with a small town in it, you cannot separate Seguin from the pecan.

Or the pecan cracker.

In addition to the aforementioned Pecan Museum of Texas, which displays a variety of pecan-cracking, -shelling, and other related equipment, Seguin is home to Pape Pecan House and Nutcracker Museum, which claims to have the world's largest collection of nutcrackers from around the world—seven thousand of them, according to John Pape.

"They're from all over the world," Pape said of the nutcrackers. "Germany. England. The Black Forest. The biggest is a man-sized nutcracker, about six feet tall."

Seguin is also home to what it bills as the world's largest pecan. At least three of them, in fact. These aren't actual pecans, of course, but rather artistic works celebrating the state's blue-ribbon tree nut. The original is a circa-1960s creation located at the Guadalupe County

A few of the featured attractions at the Pape Pecan Company's Nutcracker Museum.

The original "World's Largest Pecan" in Seguin, Texas.

courthouse. This pecan held the title of "world's largest" until an even larger pecan, reported to be twelve feet in length and weighing 12,000 pounds, was constructed in Brunswick, Missouri, in the 1980s. When news of this enormous nut reached Texas, Seguin sent a delegation to Missouri to investigate.

One member of this reconnaissance party later recalled being amused at the sight of such a large nut in a state that produces small pecans.

"It was funny because Missouri nuts are much smaller than ours, and here's this giant pecan with all these small trees around it," she told a reporter.

Meanwhile, John Pape was busy constructing a new pecan. Seeking something he could take along to parades, in 2002 he fabricated a nut even larger than the Seguin original, fitting it to an old Model A truck frame. But at this point Pape knew nothing of the big Missouri nut. When he learned of it, he began calling his creation the world's largest mobile pecan.

"Had I known about the Missouri pecan, I would have made mine bigger," Pape told me in a 2017 interview.

He would get his chance.

"These guys in Seguin pooled their money to get the title back," Pape said. "One place did the steel work. I did the wiring and connected it together. Then it was sent out for fiberglass work. Someone else painted it."

On July 4, 2011, the giant, sixteen-foot-by-eight-foot nut made its debut at Seguin's Independence Day parade, and the city reclaimed its title. And its pride.

One city official, speaking with a reporter just days before the official unveiling of the world's largest pecan, said that agriculture remains a vital part of Seguin's economy and that the big pecan symbolized the city's thriving pecan industry. She said Seguin wanted to be remembered for its pecans.

Kyle and I were discussing the possibility of using one of the refuge's boats to reach the champion pecan tree. Other than parachuting in, this seemed to be the only way to approach it.

"Are you wanting to take a picture of it?" he asked.

The thought had crossed my mind. But even the best photo wouldn't compare with getting close enough that I could actually behold the tree's great size and perhaps touch it. The only photo I wanted, I realized, was the one burned into my mind from experiencing Oklahoma's champion pecan, in person.

"I just want to see it up close," I said.

Then the wind gusted, and gusted again, stronger this time. Soon, we were looking out at a lake of whitecaps.

"When they get that big, taking the boat out can be really tricky," he said. "I hate to say it, but I don't think we'll be able to get out there today."

As disappointing as this was, I wasn't discouraged. I was going to find a way to get to the champion pecan tree. The question at this point was, what's plan D? The most obvious and practical strategy seemed to be to return in the summer, when the rains had ended and the water in the river bottom had receded. I didn't want to wait, but what choice did I have?

Later, after Kyle dropped me off at my car and returned to work, I drifted into the shade of a pecan tree where I ate my lunch. It was a large, mature specimen, and from beneath its sprawling limbs I looked out on a freshly cut meadow teeming with fluttering butterflies. A pair of bluebirds flitted through the pecan's branches, while cardinals and mockingbirds sang from the edges of the meadow. I couldn't help noticing that this pecan looked different from the wild trees back in the river bottom. This tree, though quite large, was much smaller than the natives, with a more symmetrical and uniform trunk. Perhaps a member of the Chapman family had planted the tree back when this area was part of Washita Farm, once the 13,000-acre "showplace of southern Oklahoma," according to a US Fish & Wildlife Service brochure. And every other fall—pecans are alternate-bearing trees, producing heavier yields one year and lighter crops the next—I'm sure its branches bowed with the weight of bumper crops. Even though I relished my quiet lunch beneath its expansive limbs, seeing this tree, being able to walk up and pat its heavy trunk, seemed like a consolation prize compared to the wild one I could view only from afar.

—3—

Cultivars

It's springtime, and I'm in southern Oklahoma, at the Noble Research Institute, for a seminar on pecan grafting. Not long after beginning this project I realized that if I wanted to understand the pecan industry and the production of this unique nut, I needed to study grafting. So here I am in south-central Oklahoma after driving two hours through early-morning fog so thick it reduced visibility to about a quarter mile and let up but once, in the Arbuckle Mountains, as I floated through a meadow of blooming wildflowers, an air bubble of clarity in a foggy sea, with the faint orange glow of the rising sun in the east warming my spirit, promising to burn away the hazy screen lingering all around me.

Here in Carter County the fields and pasturelands are lush and green. Trees are putting on their leaf canopies. Birds are singing. And if you slice through the bark of a pecan tree, that bark should now slip against the cambium layer, which means it's the perfect time for grafting.

Grafting is simply the process by which a shoot from one cultivar (of a variety possessing the specific characteristics the grower wants to see replicated in the grafted tree) is attached to the rootstock of another. After a period of time, the two pieces begin growing as one tree. This process allows for the cultivation of trees bearing pecans of consistent size and quality, which is essential for commercial production. The market demands crop consistency, being able to provide buyers with a steady supply of the same, high-quality pecans, season after season. Grafting is the only way to accomplish this.

A Louisiana slave named Antoine recorded the first commercially successful grafts of pecan trees in 1846, though it would be another sixty years before the practice began to gain widespread acceptance. This gave rise to the commercial pecan industry, which is still very much in its infancy. Compared to the cultivation of, say, bananas, which has been going on for thousands of years, growing pecan cultivars is a relatively new practice. But this doesn't mean these nuts haven't played an important part in our diets for thousands of years. Grant Hall's 2000 article in the journal *Economic Botany* highlights the discovery of an almost completely intact pecan nut buried at a depth of three meters in southeastern Iowa. Radiocarbon technology determined the nut was approximately 7,000 years old, though Hall writes that findings of other prehistoric pecan remains indicate that humans were using pecans long before this in the same general range in which they occur today.

At the time the pecan industry made the shift to grafting in the early 1900s, this method of propagation was already well known among growers of other tree crops. *Thomas Jefferson's Garden Book*, for example, includes several such references, including a March 31, 1773, entry documenting the grafting of five French chestnut trees into two stocks of common chestnut. A footnote explains that the latter is the American chestnut and that it was common practice in Jefferson's time to graft the European onto the American variety. In another instance, Jefferson's 1792 letter to Stephen Cathalan, American consul at Marseille, France, expressed his wish for "colonizing the olive tree to South Carolina." Jefferson wrote that the best and most economic plan for doing so would be to employ "a laboring man who understands engrafting," to grow olive trees first in Marseille for eventual import to the United States. He believed such plantings would be enhanced by grafting onto them cuttings from the most desirable trees, and he expressed his wish that young plants would be shipped each winter from Marseille to Charleston, "together with a quantity of the olive berries to be sown in Carolina in order to be engrafted on them."

In *A History of Horticulture in America to 1860*, author U. P. Hedrick writes that while many planters in the early American colonies north of Virginia grew apples and pears from seedlings, "grafted plants are mentioned so often in the South that one may suppose a large proportion of the trees of these fruits were grafted." He points to a 1746 advertisement in the *South Carolina Gazette* as typical of the time: "To Be Sold, A Choice parcel of Apple and Pear Grafts, from 1 to 3 years old." Grafting was widely practiced among European farmers, especially those in England and Holland, so it's no surprise that early colonists brought this knowledge with them to the New World. After the American Revolution this method of propagation grew in popularity as itinerant tree grafters roved across northern orchards each spring, plying their trade on apple and pear trees.

But the science of grafting goes back much farther than the settling of the New World. The great Greek botanist Theophrastus wrote about it three hundred years before Christ, describing techniques and best practices for grafting trees such as olive, fig, and pomegranate. Translations of his work reveal it to be surprisingly modern—"One must choose the proper seasons for grafting with both the country and the nature of the trees in view, since some combinations are too wet, others too dry"; "It is also reasonable that trees so grafted should bear finer fruit, especially when the scion is from a cultivated tree and the stock from a wild tree of the same bark, since the scion is better fed because the stock is strong." Theophrastus's two botanical compendiums, *Historia de Plantis* (Enquiry into Plants) and *De Causis*

Plantarum (Of Plants, an Explanation) are the greatest sources of botanical and horticultural information from antiquity, and with regard to grafting specifically, his writings on scion selection and rootstocks are viewed as the basis for modern fruit culture.

Leading today's workshop is Charles Rohla, PhD, who manages the Noble Research Institute's Center for Pecans and Specialty Agriculture. Rohla grew up on an Oklahoma farm and received his doctorate from Oklahoma State University. Dressed in work boots and Wrangler jeans, and a long-sleeved shirt, he gives the impression of someone who enjoys getting out into the orchard rather than spending all day behind a desk. He's fortyish, about six feet tall, with a powerful frame. He has closely cropped light-brown hair, mustache, and goatee, and his skin is tan from the Oklahoma sunshine.

Upon arriving at the Noble Research Institute's campus in Ardmore earlier this morning, I spotted Charles and walked over to ask him a question. I was second in line, behind a couple of older gentlemen who were peppering Rohla with queries of their own. He smiled and laughed and didn't seem to mind. When it was my turn, I stepped up and asked about an interesting cultivar I'd read about a few days earlier. "It's called the Maramec," I told him. From what I've read, it's very prolific in Oklahoma.

Rohla nodded his head and told me it had originated from a Mahan seedling in Maramec, Oklahoma. It used to be a variety that was highly recommended, but not anymore. It's proven susceptible to scab.

Ah, the dreaded pecan scab, one of the most problematic diseases affecting this nut and seemingly the bane of the industry, especially for those growers in the eastern half of the pecan belt. Scab has taken its toll on many a pecan cultivar and rendered it irrelevant or put it on the path to becoming so. I was disappointed to hear that the Maramec seemed to be one of them.

Rohla has spent more than ten years at the Noble Research Institute and has worked with pecans for a quarter century. He's an expert on, among other things, the qualities and nuances of specific cultivars. His work involves research into growing methods, increasing crop production, and identifying and evaluating new technologies to help pecan producers overcome everyday challenges. One solution offering benefits in all three of these research areas is grafting, a subject he teaches regularly. Though there are several different styles of grafting, such as the four-flap (banana) graft, the bark graft, budding, arrowhead, and the whip-and-tongue method, Rohla likes to teach techniques requiring fewer tools, which makes grafting quicker and easier.

He begins the presentation with a discussion on graft wood, the foot-long shoots of desired cultivars that will be attached to rootstocks. There are fifty or so people in attendance today, and Rohla draws our attention to a three-year-old pecan tree, a Pawnee cultivar, about twelve feet in height. He tells us it was grafted just the year before; then he points to the graft union—the line on the trunk where the graft was made. It's surprisingly low on the tree.

"From this point up," Rohla says, pointing to the graft union and lifting his finger toward the top of the tree, "that's how much this tree grew last year." Incredibly, there is approximately eight feet of this new growth! "All this," he says, "would make excellent graft wood. That's what you're looking for."

Rohla says that collecting graft wood from mature trees often results in shoots with a brown-colored cambium layer, which will likely be unsuccessful for grafting. Also, mature trees often produce growth that is too short and small in diameter to be used as graft wood. This is why new growth is preferable. What's needed is a cambium layer that's healthy and green. This is the most important part of the tree.

The discussion then moves into grafting tools, of which there is a surprising variety, ranging from long-handled loppers and pruners to saws large and small—and for some tree grafters even a staple gun.

Rohla says the most important item is a grafting knife with a sharp, straight blade, two to two-and-a-half inches in length. The next most important item? A small folding saw.

In demonstrating a variation of the Texas inlay bark graft that he calls the "American method" for the fact that it incorporates that most American of materials, duct tape, Rohla first locates a seedling tree to serve as the rootstock. He looks for a tree with a trunk less than eight inches in diameter. He says that anything larger than this will result in too much growth in too short a time, thereby undermining the union and compromising the graft. He cuts off the top of the seedling tree at a point approximately four feet above the ground. If grafting in a field where grazing livestock is present, the graft must be made much higher on the tree. Rohla says he has actually stood on the toolbox of a pickup truck to do this.

Before felling the scion, Rohla first saws through the bark on the back side of the tree in order to avoid peeling the bark from the tree once the cut is made. All it takes is a few cuts with a sharp saw, enough to slice through the bark.

Now he focuses his attention on the opposite side of the tree. He begins his cut at a point that lines up with the cut on the back of the tree, sawing until the scion is felled and then trimming any remaining pieces from the surface of the rootstock. Now, using a grafting knife, he makes a vertical cut through the bark. This cut is made at the top edge of the rootstock and extends downward on the trunk for perhaps five inches. After the cut is made, he peels back the bark at the top edge of the rootstock.

Next he prepares the scion—the graft wood, a foot-long shoot from a tree featuring the desired characteristics he wishes to duplicate in the grafted tree—by cutting an inch or so off either end in order to remove the dead wood. To do this, Rohla uses a pair of hand pruners. Then, using the grafting knife, he carves away about half the diameter of a two-inch section on the tip. As he does so, it looks like he's whittling, but he goes deeper—again, carving away about half the diameter of one end of the graft wood. This leaves a flat piece of exposed wood, two or three inches in length. This is what Rohla inserts into the rootstock. Before doing this, he makes a small cut on the back of the tip he just carved. The idea is to remove the bark so as to expose the scion's cambium layer, which must make solid contact with that of the rootstock. This cambium-to-cambium contact is vital to the integrity of the graft.

Before inserting the scion, he places it alongside the vertical cut he just made on the rootstock so that the cut aligns with one edge of the scion shoot. On the opposite edge Rohla uses the grafting knife to make another cut into the rootstock bark, basically tracing the outline of the scion. He makes this cut two to three inches—the same as the length of the scion tip to be inserted. Then he peels back the edge of the rootstock bark and inserts the tip of the scion, pushing it into the rootstock until it is snug, then tapping the shoot with the handle of his grafting knife until only a half-inch section of the exposed tip is visible. At this point nearly all the scion's carved tip has been inserted between the bark and the cambium layer of the rootstock.

Next he secures the graft with duct tape, beginning near the top of the rootstock and wrapping upward onto the scion. Now he tears the tape off the roll and presses it around the graft union so that it is completely covered. Afterward he applies duct tape to the top of the rootstock to keep it from drying out.

Rohla then peels a thin layer of duct tape from the roll and wraps it around the back side of the scion, securing it to the rootstock. Growers making numerous grafts of different varieties can use different colors of tape for this strip to help identify specific cultivars.

Now he applies a drop of Elmer's glue to the top of the scion, which prevents the shoot from drying out.

Finally, Rohla cuts a three-foot shoot from the original felled treetop and trims away the twigs. Using duct tape, he attaches this to the rootstock so that the shoot extends well above the graft. This serves as a bird perch. It helps protect the smaller, more fragile, graft.

The Pawnee seedling that Rohla referred to earlier demonstrates that grafted trees grow very quickly. And when the water and nutrients absorbed by the tree's expansive root system are directed up to a single shoot, this growth is substantial. The same is true for pruning. Reducing the number of outlets that the root system must feed accelerates the tree's upward growth.

One of the most common questions Rohla fields from those attending his grafting seminars concerns cultivars. Which varieties are best?

This depends on the specific region where they're planted. For southern Oklahoma, Rohla recommends Pawnee, which he says is early maturing and one that will bring the highest prices.

Oconee, a newer variety, is large like Pawnee but matures later in the season. Rohla says the variety known as Nocona produces a beautiful nut, and he also talks favorably about Lakota, which, he says, is currently scab resistant.

But there is another variety he likes even better: Kanza.

"It's a one-harvest tree," he says. "All the nuts fall at once. The pecans shell nicely. Last year I got two ninety a pound for mine. Kanza is a smaller nut. It has more oil and flavor than others. People buy mostly with their eyes. They like the larger nuts. But if you can get people to try Kanza, they will usually buy them."

Experimentation with different tree varieties is central to the pecan industry. There are over one thousand pecan cultivars, but only a few dozen of these are significant for today's industry. This is because older varieties often fall from favor as newer and better cultivars are developed. Growers have to weigh the advantages of each variety against its shortcomings, relative to their specific growing area, as each is essentially a compromise of some sort. For example, a specific cultivar might offer only moderate levels of disease resistance but

A pecan orchard in summer. Grafted trees such as these produce pecans of consistent size and quality.

produce mammoth-sized kernels of a beautiful golden-brown color. Some growers might tolerate its moderate levels of disease resistance in order to have the opportunity to harvest these large and very profitable kernels. Conversely, another variety might have excellent scab resistance and yet produce only a medium-sized pecan. It's a compromise. It's a trade-off. But if one lives in an area where pecan scab is particularly problematic, this compromise might make sense.

At least one newer variety blooms late (thereby avoiding late freezes) and ripens early (which limits its growing season and thus its kernel size) but offers excellent flavor and scab resistance. And for these reasons it is very popular in some parts of the pecan belt.

These are only a few examples. When it comes to pecans, there seems to be an endless array of variables by which individual cultivars are measured. And their respective advantages and corresponding value may change over time.

One of the drawbacks of growing cultivars is that they lack the natural disease resistance and hybrid vigor of their wild (native) counterparts. Consequently, growers of improved varieties, especially those in the rainy and humid Southeast, are forced to use liberal amounts of fungicides in order to control diseases such as pecan scab. And when the scab organism evolves to the point that it can resist the effects of our current fungicides, we're forced to up the ante with new concoctions, which allows us to prolong the war against scab.

This is one of the advantages of wild pecan trees. Though even these trees benefit from some management, native trees require—and typically receive—comparatively little or even no human input. The drawback is that they produce smaller pecans, which are traditionally less marketable. Still, in the pecan tree's native range many landowners are content to keep these wild trees rather than replacing them with cultivars, allowing them to produce a crop, however irregular, as a supplement to their cattle operations or other primary interests. They provide little or no management of these native trees and in many years still get a crop.

Yet, in talking to industry insiders, one marvels that there are any wild pecan trees remaining anywhere in the pecan belt. That's because the only way to produce a crop of pecans of consistent size and dependable quantity is to raise cultivars. But there's another reason that native pecan trees and the smaller, often thick-shelled, nuts they produce seem increasingly out of place in today's industry: China, whose enormous demand for these nuts has helped revive the once stagnant pecan industry. Simply put, the Chinese want the largest nuts, the kind produced by improved varieties. And they want them in copious quantities, which entices growers to employ all sorts of techniques in an attempt to mitigate the pecan's natural alternate-bearing tendency through which veritable bumper crops this year are balanced with lighter yields the next year. This is the pecan's natural survival mechanism. To moderate this (pecan farmers tell me this tree's alternate-bearing tendency can't be eliminated altogether) growers employ various management practices so as to level production and produce a more consistent supply of these nuts. Not only this, but some growers in the pecan's native range are seeking to capitalize on the nut's growing popularity and the trend toward larger pecans, and of course the higher prices they bring, by razing groves of wild trees and replacing them with improved varieties that produce the larger kernels for which many consumers, especially the Chinese, are willing to pay the highest prices. Of course, this makes us more and more dependent on chemical solutions to control disease and pests—threats that wild pecan trees developed natural resistance to over thousands of years of evolution.

As a 1995 article from the Texas A&M AgriLife Extension explains, "When man decided to select, propagate, and plant orchards with larger nut size and heavier fruiting, the natural limits of the pecan were exceeded and man's management became essential, otherwise the trees stress and die." About wild pecan trees, the article added, "One must always remember that small native nut size, alternate bearing, low yield and many other characteristics of native pecan production are a vital part of pecan survival . . . and should be considered good."

Like people in other parts of the world, Americans are growing increasingly skeptical of foods grown through the use of synthetic pesticides and fungicides. Just look at today's robust and growing organics industry. More and more we clamor for the foods that nature has provided us, grown in the very way they were intended to: naturally, organically. However, relatively few pecans on the commercial market are produced this way.

One wonders whether we will ever see an improved variety of pecan incorporating the natural vigor and disease resistance of natives while featuring the mammoth-sized kernel of today's largest cultivars. While it might seem unlikely, it certainly gives pecan scientists something to strive for. In the meantime, many are wondering whether the industry's much touted new federal marketing order will generate renewed interest in wild pecans as a result of the greater demand and correspondingly higher prices the industry predicts. If so, perhaps this could spark a native pecan revival in some parts of the pecan belt and encourage better management and conservation of existing groves of these important trees.

Why would someone choose pecans, anyway, given their soaring prices, especially considering that almonds and walnuts and pistachios and many others are so readily available, naturally nutritious, and often less costly?

Somewhere out there is a pecan grower/sheller/marketer/consumer saying to him/herself: it's for the flavor/health benefits/American pride/economic opportunity.

As demand around the world continues to rise, so do pecan prices, especially in times of reduced supply. How much higher they can go before consumers begin to eschew pecans for walnuts or almonds or something else, however, isn't clear. Hilton Segler, executive director of the National Pecan Growers Council, told me in a 2016 interview that he'd seen retail prices for shelled pecans range between $10 and $15 per pound. The industry stakeholders I spoke to throughout the pecan belt echoed this, adding that prices varied by location and retailer. When I asked a New Mexico grower how high prices could get before consumers begin seeking alternatives, he said we were getting pretty close to it now. He added that those with limited income might soon buy peanuts or skip nuts altogether.

I passed a garden center as I drove down the street yesterday in a part of town I don't often visit. The place seemed rather expansive and reasonably well stocked, so I surprised my son, Jackson, by turning into the parking lot. When I opened the door to get out, he asked if I was looking for pecan trees again. He knows me pretty well.

I'd hoped to visit with the clerk so I could ask some questions. I wanted to know things like how many pecan trees the nursery sold each season, which varieties were most popular, which ones the nursery recommends for my area. Things like that. There appeared to be only one clerk, however, and he was helping some customers inside the store. So Jackson and I looked around on our own.

We passed the greenhouse, which was filled with potted plants and hanging baskets, and headed toward the section of container trees in back of the nursery. It didn't take long to spot the pecans. They were the tallest of the nursery's tree offerings. And after conducting a quick inventory, I determined there were only three of them: a Pawnee, a Stuart, and a Cheyenne.

I would have expected the Pawnee, but the other two were surprising, especially the Stuart, the namesake of the aforementioned Col. W. R. Stuart of Ocean Springs, Mississippi, often called the "father of pecan culture." The Stuart cultivar, first offered for sale in 1892, was for most of the twentieth century probably the most popular variety planted. While there are still vast orchards of Stuart pecan trees in parts of the pecan belt, this cultivar is falling from favor with many growers and pecan scientists who no longer recommend it for new plantings. Stuart lacks something called precocity, a term that pecan farmers use to refer to a tree that begins producing at an early age. Stuart, it is frequently pointed out, may take ten to twelve years from the time it is planted to produce a significant crop of nuts. Conversely, some other cultivars take only eight years to produce a similar yield.

And then there's the issue of the nut itself. Many insist that Stuart produces only a marginal-quality, low-percentage kernel. Stuart struggles to fill well, which means this variety is not as efficient at filling the shell with kernel as are some other cultivars. Thus, for each pecan produced, Stuart provides slightly less kernel and more empty space.

If you have a Stuart tree in your backyard and you gather the nuts each autumn for Thanksgiving and Christmas pies and other goodies, you might not notice or care. If, on the other hand, you own an enterprise with ten thousand trees, this difference can be significant.

While Stuart's popularity is beginning to fade, Pawnee is a variety that continues to find favor with growers. This is a newer cultivar that's becoming extremely popular across the pecan belt. It's noted for its large kernel and a tendency for early maturing, which allows growers to get their crops into the market early for the best prices. Many pecan farmers insist that if you're looking to make the most money from your orchard, Pawnee is the cultivar you want.

It's so good that at least one nursery calls Pawnee the most planted pecan in North America today, citing its heavy production two to three weeks ahead of other varieties.

When Hurricane Irma moved through Georgia as a downgraded, though still formidable, tropical storm in September 2017, it destroyed thousands of trees across the state. These trees were extremely vulnerable due to the pecan crop they carried, which made them unstable in Irma's high winds. Early reports placed the loss at 30 percent of the state's annual crop. Even for the nation's leader in pecan production, a state that produces, in some years, one hundred million pounds, this is significant, especially considering that US production averages only about 280 million pounds per year.

At the time of Irma's arrival in Georgia, most varieties of pecans were still weeks away from harvest. The state's Pawnee pecans, however, were fully ripened, and their shucks were opening. As a result, many of them were able to be salvaged.

The feedback was overwhelmingly positive. Comments included, "Excellent product, fast reliable service" and "Great to do business with—would buy again." Perhaps most intriguing was a comment that read, simply, "Fast shipping, good seeds." With hundreds of successful transactions to his credit, I realized this was my kind of seller.

The item piquing my curiosity was a handful—or maybe two handfuls—of pecans. They were advertised on eBay as "2017 Iowa Northern Pecan nuts seeds (20 seeds)." I was intrigued in part because the nuts appeared to be from northern-strain trees, in this case from Iowa, which constitutes the pecan's traditional northern limit. The seller's description noted that these seeds were from a small town roughly 160 miles north of Davenport, Iowa, which is typically referenced as the pecan's northernmost latitude. Davenport's location along the Mississippi River was always conducive for pecan trees, although many of the wild stands of these trees have been bulldozed and replaced with crops such as corn. And yet here was an eBay listing for twenty pecan seeds, fresh from the 2017 harvest, grown from trees located a mere twenty miles from Iowa's border with Minnesota where, according to the seller, winter lows average ten to twenty degrees below zero.

My interest in these particular pecans went beyond the fact that the trees that had produced them grew in such a northerly clime, but more importantly that they had produced nuts at all. After all, Thomas Jefferson once wrote to a friend in New Orleans, complaining that his twenty-year-old pecan trees on his Monticello estate in Virginia had not yet produced fruit. His friend replied that perhaps they'd been planted in too elevated a location, as in his region these trees began producing much sooner, in eight or ten years. Perhaps Monticello's elevated latitude, if not the specific varieties planted, had something to do with it. A pecan scientist recently told me of a small orchard of these trees growing in Canada. It's unclear how prolific they are, although they would be smaller than their southern counterparts given their limited growing season. Indeed, the eBay description for the 2017 Iowa pecans explained that these twenty seeds were smaller than southern pecans, with kernels the size of hickory nuts. The seller noted that most of the nuts dropped over the course of a week, with one tree releasing 600 in one night.

Of course, this was exactly what the region's native pecan trees have been doing over the course of thousands of years: dropping pecans onto the river bottom soils from which they themselves grew, some of which were eaten by squirrels and crows, and some of which germinated and took root in these fertile, well-drained soils. From these neglected or overlooked pecans, seedlings grew and eventually developed into mature trees. True to the pecan's nature, each was genetically distinct. Many of these trees, perhaps most of them, eventually succumbed to the area's severe winters, which are in this northerly latitude frequent and inevitable. Others fell to disease. A few survived, however, and from these survivors more nuts fell, germinated, took root, and developed into seedlings. Eventually, over hundreds of years, over thousands of years, the success rate of these seedling trees improved as evolution slowly but inevitably favored those hardy trees whose genetics permitted them to somehow withstand the region's long, harsh, unforgiving winters and short growing seasons. These specially adapted, resilient trees eventually formed the northern reaches of the pecan's native range, a range modestly expanded through the natural process of herbivory and also by American Indians, who are believed to have planted pecan trees along frequently traveled waterways and campsites—something they are also believed to have done with other native tree crops such as the pawpaw.

While many of these traditional stands of pecan trees eventually fell to agriculture and development, a 1979 article in the *Mother Earth News* explained that a few of these resilient old "Indian orchards" had been discovered as far north as southern Wisconsin and in the northernmost regions of Iowa and Illinois, hidden away in rugged forests, overlooked or forgotten. By the time the article appeared, delegates from the Northern Nut Growers Association (NNGA) had already made exploratory visits into this, the far northern reaches of the pecan, to collect seeds from these surviving trees. Shortly thereafter, the NNGA established a distribution program with the intention of preserving, and even expanding, the remaining population of these northern-strain trees before they were all lost to development. These collected seeds were packaged and offered along with growing instructions to new NNGA members. In return, the NNGA requested that recipients complete occasional questionnaires in succeeding years about the performance of their pecan trees.

It is unclear to what extent, if any, the program expanded populations of these northern-strain pecans. The NNGA's Tucker Hill told me that the seed program lasted for only one year and that resulting data was never collected as the organization simply lacked the resources. Hill said membership in the NNGA nearly doubled, however, and that the evaluation of these native northern pecan trees led to the development of some excellent cultivars, perhaps such as those isolated pecans in Canada.

But it was wild pecan trees I was most interested in, and in this case those remaining stands of native, northern trees. I wondered how many remained. This, too, was unclear, although I was able to locate someone who had successfully grown pecan trees from seeds distributed by the NNGA program in 1979–1980. He lived in northeast Iowa, a mere twenty miles from that state's border with Minnesota, and he was selling seeds from these trees on eBay. After thirty-five years, his item description explained, his trees were thirty-five feet tall. The year before, three of these trees had each produced over 1,000 nuts. In keeping with the spirit of the NNGA program nearly forty years earlier, he was providing instructions on how to start the seeds in four-inch-diameter tubes, how to protect the seedlings from squirrels and raccoons, and finally how to transfer these seedlings from container to ground the following year. The photos accompanying the listing included images of the pecan nuts themselves, as well as trays of seedlings, and even shots of the mature pecan trees that had produced the seeds. I was sold.

While I certainly didn't need the seeds, and though they wouldn't be a fit for my growing region on the southern Great Plains, where our winters are often mild and our summers almost always long and scorching, I clicked "Buy it Now" because I have family in the Midwest. Weeks later, as I addressed to them the envelope containing these northern pecans and planting instructions, I realized I was continuing, in a minor way, the effort undertaken by the Northern Nut Growers Association in 1979 and the American Indian planters of hundreds of years ago.

—4—

Pecans for Sale

I'm visiting with the owner of a specialty food store in Norman, Oklahoma, a store he refers to as the Nut House. Its products include not just pecans but all sorts of nuts, including almonds, walnuts, peanuts, pine nuts, macadamia nuts, cashews, pistachios, Brazil nuts, and even Spanish peanuts. But the star of the shelves, and the nut most popular with customers, according to the proprietor, is the pecan, which the store stocks in many varieties. These may fluctuate year to year, but they typically include Elliott from the southeastern United States and Kanza, Mohawk, Pawnee, Caddo, Major, and natives from Oklahoma. These pecans are offered shelled or unshelled, in halves or pieces, or in the form of finely ground meal (often called pecan flour). They're packaged in shiny sixteen-ounce bags, and in three-, five-, and ten-pound sacks. Some varieties are offered in thirty-pound cases. They're available raw or roasted, salted or unsalted, or candy-coated with honey or coconut or chocolate or caramel or butterscotch or maple or other delectable flavors. Additionally, pecans are offered as ingredients in some of the store's other products, such as pies, breads, cookies, candy bars, pralines, brittles, chocolate-covered nut clusters, fudge, and nut mixes, or pressed and squeezed and filtered and available in the form of pecan oil, a product that is currently out of stock.

Such breadth and depth and variety of pecan products shouldn't come as any surprise whatsoever considering the name of the store, which is Mason's Pecans, established by Bill and Karen Mason in 1967 and operated today by second-generation owner Brett Mason, who often refers to himself as the store's Head Nut, a title he includes in his e-mail signature.

I grew up in Norman and lived there for eighteen years before leaving for California and the Marine Corps in 1988. Norman is a very small city, a college town, and naturally I knew about Mason's Pecans; I must have passed by the establishment dozens of times during my childhood. For some reason, however, I never visited. I don't know why.

With the store's glass-door cooler and miniature aisles and pecan-packed shelves, it reminds me vaguely of the old-fashioned neighborhood markets I remember from my childhood, tiny screen-doored grocery stores that I'd walk to, or ride my bike to, for bread and milk, or if I was lucky, a cream soda and a Marathon candy bar. And then there's Brett, who seems to know everything about every product in his store, and pecans in general. Ask him a question about the current crop, for example, and he may respond with something approximating this: *Man, I'm swimming in nuts. I'm getting two thousand pounds a week. This is the best pecan crop we've had since 2013, which was a special year because . . .*

When Brett was seven years old, his father decided to get into the pecan-cracking business. He didn't own a cracking machine at this point, so he served as an intermediary for customers who wanted to have their pecans processed. They would drop them off at the Mason home, and on weekends Bill would take them to Ada to have them cracked. Customers would return the following week to collect their pecans.

Brett Mason is the second-generation owner of Mason's Pecans, the Norman, Oklahoma, retail store and custom-shelling business begun by his parents, Bill and Karen Mason, in 1967.

In 1968 Bill bought an antique cracking machine. He quickly realized this machine couldn't keep pace with demand, however, so he took out a signature loan to buy additional equipment from the estate of a farmer in nearby Tecumseh. He added three crackers, a sheller, and a blower to his inventory. The Masons advertised by distributing flyers to homes with pecan trees in the yard or by stapling them to telephone poles.

"That year we did gangbusters," Brett recalls. "We did really well."

Brett is fifty-eight but looks ten years younger, a result perhaps of genetics, his proclivity for organic foods, or his decades living as an islander, first on St. Thomas in the Caribbean and then on Maui, Hawaii, where he thrived for twenty years before returning to Norman to take over the family business after his father's passing. Though today landlocked, he retains an islander's spirit, wearing a Hawaiian fish-hook necklace and a glinting stud in his left ear. His gaze is intelligent, energetic, and ocean-blue as he talks of future adventures, such as sailing his twenty-five-foot, swing-keeled sailboat back to the Hawaiian islands.

"People have sailed around the world on boats smaller than this," he says. "I just need to experiment a bit more with that swing keel. It's great for shallow water, getting into rivers and coves, but it needs more testing in big water before I take on the ocean."

It wouldn't be his first daring excursion. Two weeks before completing his junior year of high school, in May of 1976, Brett and a friend talked their parents and high school principal into letting them out of school early so they could ride their bicycles to the desert Southwest.

"They didn't want to let us," Brett says," but we convinced them that we needed to leave two weeks early to keep from burning up."

They reached Madill, in southern Oklahoma—a distance of over 100 miles—the first night. When they arrived at the city park, thunderstorms were brewing overhead. Brett and his friend had no tent. They were considering taking shelter beneath a picnic table when some kids in an MG pulled up and asked what they were doing. Brett told them, and the kids returned a short while later in a pickup truck, offering to let the pair stay with their grandparents. Brett says they loaded their bikes into the truck, and after getting to the house and moving their gear inside, they changed clothes and headed off with their new friends to a keg party. The next morning, the grandparents cooked Brett and his buddy a big, country breakfast.

"We were treated really well during the trip," Brett tells me.

Six weeks later they'd covered 2,700 miles, both as bicycle riders and as grateful passengers in the automobiles of the several people who stopped to give them rides. But Brett was just getting started. A few years later, he and another friend circumnavigated North America by hitchhiking, going from Norman to Los Angeles, then to Vancouver, Montreal, down to Key West and back to Oklahoma.

"I've hitchhiked quite a bit," Brett says. "I could hitchhike across the US faster than you could drive it, practically."

In 1983 he quit college, packed his bags, and rode off on his motorcycle toward the Caribbean, telling himself that if things didn't work out he could sell the bike to get back home. He would stay gone for twenty-two years.

We move into Brett's office, our conversation veering back and forth between sailing and motorcycles, and occasionally pecans. It's essentially a corner closet, a hidden room of sorts, with a window looking out onto the front counter. Brett's desk is covered in stacks of papers and two computer monitors. On the wall behind me is a map of Oklahoma. On the wall opposite the desk is a dry-erase board. On this board is a to-do list:

Paint Mason's on Building
Sanitize all coolers
Get animal food cooler done

One thing I've noticed as I visit with Brett is the constant stream of customers who come into the store. They've trickled in steadily, one every fifteen minutes or so, young and old, men and women, individuals as well as couples, making purchases of a single item or multiple items, some of whom are in and out quickly, and others who stay and talk to Maran, the woman running the cash register.

Others, especially in the fall, bring Brett pecans—bags of them, boxes of them, feed sacks brimming with them. Mason's Pecans specializes in cracking and shelling its namesake nuts for small growers. Often, they're not farmers at all but people who simply happen to have a few pecan trees in their yards. In autumn, when the nuts fall from the trees, they gather them and bring them to Mason's Pecans for shelling, ideally after first cleaning out the sticks and stones and other debris that can damage the expensive shelling machinery. The pecans are weighed, and a claim ticket is issued. When they're ready to be picked up, the staff calls the customer.

"Last year we didn't get many pecans," Brett tells me. "I don't know why. The experts tell me the trees were stressed. I'm like, *What* stress? They're *trees!*"

"For the store," he says, "we buy pecans from local growers, mostly, but sometimes from out of state when we can't get enough of them here. We started as a seasonal business, doing custom pecan shelling, which meant we were closed during the summer. The retail store opened in 1983. We wanted to stay open during the summer, so we opened the store and purchased a roaster so we could roast our own nuts. Our customers are from all over the state, even people from out of state just passing through. A lot of people come down from the North to spend winter on the Gulf. As they head back home, they stop by and buy a year's supply of pecans. They do this every year."

"I had a client who used to buy my pecans for his fried-pie business. Then he said he found a cheaper source. I told him they were probably old. I said enjoy them while they last. He said they were. They soon went rancid on him. But he saved money for a short time."

Brett says you have to know what you're buying. Sometimes people cut their pecans into pieces to hide the dark color and imperfections. When they're cut, the white seams give the impression that the kernels are lighter in color, which is more desirable.

"We sell organic pecans, but I have a hard time keeping them in stock. Lots of growers don't want to do this. From central Oklahoma east they have to use insecticides and fungicides to control pests and diseases. The growers in the west don't have to do this as much. It's about the same cost to grow organic and sacrifice some volume as it is to spray and pay."

"A lot of customers like the native pecans," Brett says. "They have to know about them. Some don't. Those from Oklahoma or Texas usually do, and they'll ask for natives. They have a higher oil content, and they taste better than the others. Since it started raining again the last few years they haven't been quite as good. They're still really good, but not quite as good as they usually are. During the drought years they were the best. Another one customers really like is the Kanza. They're planting a lot of Kanza in Oklahoma, especially in northern Oklahoma. It was developed for Kansas and northern Oklahoma. The tree buds later in the year, so it misses late freezes, and the nuts ripen earlier. The growing season is shorter for Kanza, so it's a smaller nut. But people really like them. We also sell a lot of Pawnee. It's a popular variety in Oklahoma. It's bigger than Kanza. And I've been bringing some Elliotts in from the Southeast. You can't grow Elliotts here. The tree buds too early in the year. It's susceptible to frost. People really like them. Elliotts have a higher oil content. Not as high as the natives, but more than most. And they have a nice sweet kernel."

"Those in the back there are bagged as squirrel or wildlife feed. That just means they've fallen on the ground or something, or they've sat too long. So we bag them up and sell them for bird feed or squirrel feed. We usually sell out of the last year's crop by the time the next crop comes in. What I can't sell I market as squirrel or bird feed. They don't seem to mind."

"We have specific growers we buy from, but I've had people come in with bags of pecans they've gathered up from their yard, or with their trunks full of pecans, telling me they need to sell them for Christmas money, that these nuts are all they have to make money with for Christmas. And I have bought them to help them out. I couldn't sell them [for human consumption] because I didn't know where the nuts had been, so I bagged them up and sold them as squirrel food."

At one point Brett excuses himself and returns a few minutes later with a Tupperware bowl full of mixed nuts—almonds and macadamia nuts seasoned with chili pepper and garlic—which he offers and I gladly accept. I notice no pecans in the mix, although there are some plump cashews. Brett tells me they're from Tanzania. They are excellent.

"I just read a market update on cashews," he says. "Prices, they already went up twice. It looks like they're going to go up again. Almonds are going to stabilize and possibly come down a little bit in price."

"Do you like pecans?" I ask.

He laughs and admits he eats more cashews and almonds. "I eat a lot of cashews right now and I'm trying to cut back on them," he says. "These two [almonds and cashews] are what I mainly eat. During the season, when I'm processing them, I'm always eating pecans."

"Being that I lived in Maui, where there's a pretty educated population on food, everybody wanted organic or as natural as was possible. I come here and bring in organic pecans, and people look at me like I'm crazy. As more and more people come to wake up and realize what's happening with their food and wondering why their health stinks . . . by and large it's what we're eating. Our stomach is a biome, a life force that needs to be maintained."

"In the past the person who would come in to buy pecans was usually someone who liked to cook," he says. "We're getting a lot more people now that just want to eat pecans. Snack on them."

"A lot of times this is my lunch," he says, referring to the bowl of nuts in his hand. "Just nuts. A lot of times it's my dinner. I get off work. I'm tired and think, what am I gonna do? It's easy: beer, nuts, computer, check my e-mail, daydream about sailing around the world."

"Are you going back to Hawaii?"

"Yeah," he says. "I would like to take this boat. It's not quite big enough. But gosh that swing keel just lets me get into places you normally wouldn't be able to get into. I do want to get down to the Lower Antilles chain. I definitely want to get to Chile. On the western side of the mountains are bays back in there that are supposedly really wonderful. And I would like to go to Antarctica. And Alaska. There are people there who live on their boat. They go to work and come home to their boat. I've always wanted to spend at least two years in Alaska. Experience two complete cycles."

Once found primarily in the South Central United States, pecan trees now grow in every southern and southwestern state, from Florida to California. This fact, and the degree to which cultivated trees have expanded the pecan industry, are perhaps best realized in Georgia, which leads the nation in pecan production despite the fact that the Peach State is outside the tree's native range. Georgia's current 140,000 acres of bearing trees produce an average of 95 million pounds of pecans annually, easily outpacing New Mexico and Texas, the next most prolific pecan-producing states. How valuable are all these nuts? A 2016 report from the Center for Agribusiness and Economic Development at the University of Georgia ranked pecans ninth on its list of the state's top agricultural commodities, with a value of $355 million, nearly $80 million more than Georgia's top vegetable commodity—corn—and $307 million more than the state's famous peaches.

This may rankle some in Texas, a traditional pecan powerhouse and the place where some believe America's indigenous tree nut originated in antiquity. Indeed, various rivalries persist today within the pecan belt, especially between Georgia and Texas. Those in the Lone Star State have been known to point out that Georgia has no native pecans, and that its trees were imported from Texas. Meanwhile, Georgia revels in its continued production dominance and also through an occasional jab of its own.

Consider, for example, the historical marker in St. Marys, a tiny seaport town in Georgia's far southeastern corner. It reads, "First Pecan Trees Grown Here about 1840." According to the sign, erected

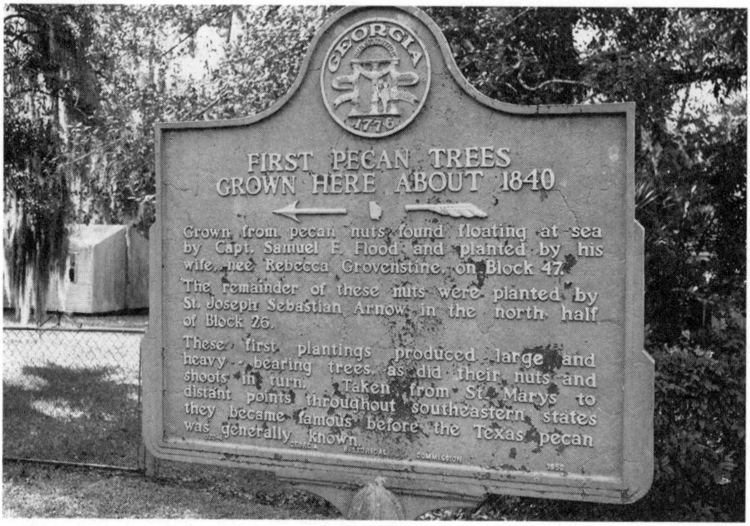

Historic pecan-tree sign in St. Marys, Georgia.

by the Georgia Historical Commission in the 1950s, these trees were grown from pecan seeds found floating at sea. They produced large, prolific trees, the nuts and shoots of which were distributed throughout the southeastern United States. This, as the marker reads, helped these Georgia trees become famous "before the Texas pecan was generally known."

Having lived on the southern plains for most of my life, in the states of Oklahoma and Texas, I know what a grove of native pecan trees looks like. Some of the most peaceful and pleasant landscapes in this part of the country are those bucolic bottoms alongside rivers and streams where wild pecans grow in abundance. But given Georgia's status as the top pecan-producing state, and considering that it's well outside the pecan's native range, I had to see for myself what a Peach State pecan operation looks like.

In the summer of 2016, I travelled to Brunswick, Georgia, an historic coastal city noted for its forest of live-oak trees, whose sprawling branches and seemingly continuous leaf canopy shade street after street of elegant Victorian homes in a warm, subtropical climate and relaxed atmosphere that are very much to my liking. Brunswick was not my destination, however, but rather the starting point for my Georgia adventure, and while there I had the good fortune to see a particularly distinguished tree known locally as the Lover's Oak, a live-oak tree that's believed to be over 900 years old. There must be hundreds or even thousands of centuries-old live oaks in this coastal community, and finding the Lover's Oak wasn't easy. I stopped and inquired of an old man who was walking his dog. He managed to guide me to the vicinity of this famous tree. Then, a few blocks nearer, I stumbled upon a neighborhood deli, whose soft-spoken proprietor—gently chiding me for ordering unsweetened iced tea, saying, "This is the South, man. We like our tea sweet"—pointed me to the exact intersection where the sprawling tree stood, where even the street deferred to its generous and utterly distinguished trunk, weaving around either side of the stately oak. Though the city's live oaks are part of a larger maritime forest that blankets much of coastal Georgia and northeastern Florida (and into the Carolinas), and though these graceful Southern trees are found throughout Brunswick, making it difficult to identify one specific specimen, once I spotted the Lover's Oak—so named because Indian braves are said to have met their maidens beneath these powerful, sprawling branches—there was no doubt it was the correct one. Majestic trees, whether live oaks or pecans, have their own unique way of communicating their significance. I stood on the sidewalk and beheld the massive tree from a short distance, then from beneath its branches, which spread over and across the street on either side of its trunk and which bore so many Spanish moss beards it was as if a community of wizards resided within. Finally, I walked up and patted its heavy trunk and felt the live oak's unmistakable permanence and solidity. I was humbled to find myself in the sweet, graceful shade of so distinguished and magnificent a tree. Live-oak trees are breathtaking, and this one, the Lover's Oak, was spectacular.

But it was pecans I'd come for, and it was pecans that called me away as I headed west from the Georgia coast, through a landscape of towering pines and quiet, bucolic fields. I was nearly to Waycross, an hour away from Brunswick, before I spotted the first pecan trees, a tall pair shading a farmhouse just off the highway. Pecans became gradually more common the farther west I traveled, appearing now in neat orchards and gracing fields and country lawns. In a small town I passed a convenience store with a sign advertising, not beer and cigarettes, not milk and bread, but "Music and Pecans." I continued west, eventually reaching the small city of Tifton, where I spotted another store whose roof featured two prominent signs. The first read "Peanuts." The second sign was much larger and featured, in capital letters, the word "PECANS." When I asked the proprietor which varieties the company grows, she told me the business does not grow any pecans but rather buys them from local farmers. "Right now we have Schleys and Elliotts mostly," she said. Then, still thinking about the two signs outside and cognizant of Georgia's reputation as a peanut-producing state, I asked the woman if she sold more pecans than peanuts. "Yes," she said. "Sometimes."

Later, in southwest Georgia, I turned off the highway and made my way along one country road after another where I encountered very little traffic other than a few farm trucks and tractors, various country churches, and the occasional quail plantation. As I entered Dougherty County, often called the "pecan capital of the world" for its incredibly vast acreage of pecan trees, the few open fields I passed seemed forgotten, for the surrounding landscape was absolutely dominated by pecans. They were everywhere, planted in perfect rows, neatly spaced and with the bare ground exposed around the base of their trunks such that each tree appeared to have a dirt pedestal holding it upright. Actually, as one grower later told me, the practice of removing all grass, weeds, and competing vegetation from around the base of the trunk allows a tree to absorb all available moisture and nutrients, nourishment passed on to the pecans. When I passed a sign that read "Pecan City," I knew I'd come to the right place. This area features what some believe is the state's largest continuous block of pecan trees—so many that one is said to be able to walk nearly five miles in a single direction without ever leaving the shade of these wonderful pecan trees. Just around the corner, on Willson Road, I found Sunnyland Farms, where I parked my car in the shade of the pecan-tree canopy. Then I walked through the gate and into the nearest of several outbuildings that formed something of a small industrial complex. Here I met Sunnyland's chief marketing officer, a woman named Teresa Barbre, who was expecting me.

Teresa was like an old friend. Her smile and genuine demeanor put me at ease, and she absolutely loved telling me about Sunnyland Farms and its 1,300 acres of pecans. She was most enthusiastic and had much to say about the company and its history.

Sunnyland Farms grows Schley, Elliott, and Desirable varieties, cultivars that produce the top-grade pecans for which the company is known. These pecans are shipped to customers across the United States, including some politicians, actors, and philanthropists, and were once sent regularly to the White House. Teresa told me that policy changes regarding gifting, as well as heightened security in recent years, have curtailed this tradition. In addition to its famous, extra-fancy mammoth pecan halves, Sunnyland Farms sells a multitude of pecan-related candies and baked goods, all produced on-site in the farm's squeaky-clean bakery. As Teresa guided me from the cleaning and grading facility into the shelling house, where pecans are cracked and separated, to the packing room, and finally into the kitchen, the warm, sweet scent of baked goods permeated the air. On the day I was there, the kitchen staff was preparing small fruitcakes, some of which sat cooling on large baking sheets while dozens of others rotated inside Sunnyland Farms's new, state-of-the-art industrial oven, which Teresa delighted in telling me about.

"It took us a long time to decide to make the investment," she said, "but we're so happy we did. Look at it. It's wonderful."

And it was. So was all the equipment. Each year the production machinery is broken down, cleaned, and repainted in order to keep everything in tip-top shape. Everywhere we went, the machinery and facilities were clean, well maintained, and managed by employees who smiled when they saw Teresa.

In the packing room there was a team of eight women standing around a conveyor belt blanketed in tiny pecan pieces. Two of the women looked up and smiled as we approached. The conveyor was vibrating, keeping the pecan pieces in constant motion. It reminded me of the electric football game I played with as a child. When plugged into the electrical outlet, the green field would vibrate noisily, which set the tiny players into motion, resulting in a play from scrimmage. As I recall, keeping track of the ball carrier amid this animated, buzzing frenzy could be tricky, but it presented nowhere near the challenge that these women faced in sorting through the miniscule pecan pieces. And yet they seemed undaunted as their hands deftly picked out the errant fragments, which to my inexperienced eyes looked exactly like the others.

"They're removing the pieces that don't have the right color," Teresa said, elevating her voice over the droning conveyor belt. "Even these tiny pecan pieces have to meet our quality standards."

Up to this point the pecan-processing procedure is mechanized, beginning with the tree shakers that dislodge nuts from the trees, to the sweepers that collect them from the ground, to the cleaning, and to the shelling. Yet, the final quality-control step before packaging is trusted only to human eyes, that team of sharp-eyed women convened around the conveyor belt. Those pecan pieces that pass their scrutiny are packed, thirty pounds to a box, and shipped around the United States to manufacturers of ice cream and candy.

Sunnyland Farms continues its long tradition of conducting business through mail order—the company also accepts orders through its website—and produces an annual catalog featuring its many products. Teresa told me that 80 percent of the farm's annual sales are completed during a twelve-week period in late fall, a time coinciding with both the holiday season and pecan harvest. The company employs nearly fifty full-time employees who handle everything from planting, maintenance, and care of the pecan orchard, to cleaning, shelling, and processing the nuts, as well as producing its numerous food products. Temporary workers are hired to assist during the hectic harvest season.

As streamlined and organized as the Sunnyland Farms production facilities were, what I most noticed was the immense orchard, row after row of pecan trees, generously spaced to allow ample sunlight exposure and air flow between branches. As pecan trees grow, they require greater space between individual trees. Some growers plant trees close together in order to take full advantage of available space, and then remove, say, every other tree once they reach a certain size. Sometimes even mature trees are relocated. During my visit to Sunnyland Farms, Teresa pointed out an excavating machine that pulled even large trees out of the ground, allowing workers to move them.

It was obvious that every aspect of the farm's pecan operation had been carefully considered and planned so as to produce a very specific result. Nothing was left to chance; every aspect of production was cultivated, nurtured, and managed by human hands in order to achieve the desired outcome. And this was only one farm. Today's pecan industry is based on exactly this type of innovation, even in traditional pecan-producing states where native pecans figure into the annual harvest. But after my visit to Georgia, which leads the nation in the production of a crop that doesn't naturally occur there, I began to wonder about the value of a wild crop when humans can manufacture one that's bigger and maybe even better.

Opening Day: My wife and I arrive at the Couch Orchard in Luther, Oklahoma, at 9:50 a.m. We turn off the section road and drive through an open gate where a sign reads "Pecan Sales Nov 15–Jan 1." We're ten minutes early, and already there are dozens of cars parked in the orchard, ranging from Jaguar luxury coupes to enormous pickups and SUVs. Up ahead, clusters of people are standing around the metal building where the pecans are processed and sold. An attendant approaches our car and greets us. She hands me a poker chip featuring the number 37 on either side. She tells us to pull into the orchard and park, that we can either wait in our car or enjoy the café around the corner. "When your number is called, it will be your time to buy pecans," she says. "We'll let you know."

We drive into the orchard, past rows of cars and people sitting inside their cars. An attendant in an orange vest directs us to our parking space beneath a large pecan tree. As I park the car, leaves dislodged by the morning breeze fall onto my car's hood like confetti celebrating the fruitful season just ended. There seem to be eight or ten attendants posted around the orchard and parking area, and they all sport blaze-orange vests of the type that deer hunters wear. I'm not certain whether deer are in season, but judging by the loud booming sounds in the near distance, coming from all around us, it seems hunting for something or another is happening and the action fast and steady. Every time I hear a boom I instinctively flinch and look over my shoulder. But I see no hunters.

"Those are the cannons," says the girl at the front gate a short while later. Everyone calls her Red. She has long, thick, red hair and wears a pair of tight-fitting jeans and tall rubber boots. Her fingers are

November 15 is Opening Day at the Couch Pecan Orchard in Luther, Oklahoma, where consumers gather for the opportunity to purchase fresh pecans.

stained from handling pecans. "They're set up all around the orchard to keep crows away."

I tell myself they must be marauding the pecan crop because the cannons are going off every few seconds, to the north, to the west, and the south. In between booms, crows are cawing in the distance. Now a blue jay calls. I spot the bird flying through the trees. Crows seem to be the nemesis of every pecan farmer I've spoken to, but blue jays take their share of these delicious nuts as well. Red says that along with the cannons, they use eagle calls to rid the orchard of crows. If any eagles are calling, I can't hear them for the cannons and the noise from traffic driving by out on Route 66 and the throngs of cars pulling into the orchard.

There is a sign erected near the front gate featuring prices for shelled and unshelled pecans. A couple of men wander up to inspect it. They tell us they've driven here from Oklahoma City. When my wife asks them if they're going to make pies with their pecans, one of the men snorts and shakes his head. "Humph," he says, as if this is the last thing anyone would do with pecans. "We're not making pies," he says. "We're going to sit and watch football and eat pecans."

Cars continue to funnel through the open gate, each driver stopping to take a poker chip before proceeding into the orchard. Now one of the other staff members walks up to the gate. I ask which variety of pecans is most popular. He thinks about it a moment and says the smaller pecans have more oil and a better flavor. Then he adds, "I think 'Maramec' is my favorite, though."

Red must have eaten her pecans for breakfast because she's full of energy, darting back and forth between her station and the cars crowding into the orchard. A dump truck passing by out on the road lets loose with a couple of blasts on its air horn. I ask Red if she has worked in the orchard long, and she admits it is her first year, although she comes from a farming background. She says she's the only female among the harvesting crew. Her job is following the tree shakers and sweeping the pecans away from the tree trunks so that the harvesters can collect them off the ground. I ask her what this is like, and she replies that it's hard work, harder in fact than any other farming-related work she's ever done. "But I love it out here," she says. "I'd much rather be out here than indoors."

Now a car approaches the gate driving in the opposite direction, leaving the orchard. The driver rolls down the passenger window and hands Red her poker chip. "I don't want to wait all day, says an elderly woman. "I think I'll come back when the crowd thins out."

I don't know how long we've been waiting to buy pecans, but we're already here and have a number. As far as I'm concerned, we're all in. So I just enjoy the warm, breezy morning in the pecan orchard.

Standing beside the door to the metal building where the pecans are processed, and beneath a sign that reads "Pecan Sales," is a tall, rangy man wearing a pair of striped overalls. Every now and then he leans down to write something on a small dry-erase board. Then he straightens and lifts this board overhead, slowly twisting left and right so that the crowd gathered around, as well as those still in their cars in the orchard, can see which numbers are being served. Currently it is 5–10.

An older gentleman appears at the front gate and studies the prices listed on the sign. He looks at me and asks whether he can buy pecans in smaller quantities than the five- or ten-pound lots advertised. I admit that I don't know, that it is our first Opening Day. Then my wife asks the man what he intends to use the pecans for. Pies? Cookies?

"My wife sent me up here," the man says. "I don't know what she uses them for."

We leave the front gate and make our way toward the metal warehouse where one of the men in orange vests is giving a group of customers a lesson on pecan processing. "First you have to separate them by variety," he says. "If you adjust the cracking machine for a small one, and then run a big one through it, it'll pulverize it. So you have to separate them."

A woman standing nearby offers that she's from Colorado and this is her second time experiencing Opening Day. "We normally mail order them," she says. "But since we're here in person this year we'll be able to buy extra pecans for the price we normally pay for shipping."

I ask the woman what's so good about these pecans. I ask why she stands in line to buy something she can easily buy in a store. "They're fresh!" she says without hesitation. Then she smiles and tells us that you have to be careful what you buy in the grocery store. "If they sit too long on the shelves, they're not any good. Don't buy the dark ones," she says. "Those are the bad ones."

"Ten to fifteen," bellows the tall man at the front door, holding the dry-erase board overhead amid the background booming of cannon fire. Leaves, dislodged by the warm November breeze, flutter to the ground, showering the convivial crowd with organic confetti.

Customers file out of the store with their purchases, holding five- and ten-pound bags of pecans in their hands and arms. Some leave the store carrying grocery bags stuffed with these smaller sacks. Several customers have staff members carrying the pecans for them, like grocery stores used to do. One customer has purchased eighty pounds of shelled pecans and has them wheeled out to his car on a dolly. The brown paper bags are already beginning to darken from the absorbed pecan oil. "See you next year," he says.

As we stand around talking with some of the other customers, I hear a hollow ticking noise coming from the east end of the building, where a grain bin is situated. "Those are pecan shells being funneled into the bin," says a bearded man in a blaze-orange vest. "We sell them as mulch. They're great for your flower beds. Termites don't like them."

A little over an hour after our arrival, the man calls our number, and we enter the pecan store where three women stand around manning stations. One table has a stack of Pawnee pecans in brown paper bags, and another table features clear plastic bags of shelled Kanza pecans. I ask one of the women if they have any Meramec, but it seems these are unavailable at the moment. So we buy a bag of Pawnees and a bag of Kanzas, and as we leave the building say goodbye to several new friends we've made among the crowd standing outside the store—people who know that Opening Day comes around but once a year and that it's not every orchard that grows America's native tree nut alongside America's Mother Road, Route 66.

One day last winter I was sitting in the José Martí International Airport just outside Havana, Cuba, when I was informed that my plane, which was coming from Venezuela, was delayed. Of course, this was going to delay my flight to Miami as well. I'd skipped breakfast that morning, and now I was getting hungry. All around me travelers were walking by carrying boxes of Cuban cigars and bottles of Havana Club rum. As for me, I was content in knowing my Cuban coffee was safe in my bag. Every now and then I'd open the briefcase for something or other and smile when I noticed that my tropical coffee grounds weren't leaking out all over my travel documents.

Later, growing hungrier still, I was glancing at the menu for the airport's single food station when a woman sitting at my table remarked that if our travels were going to be delayed, we might as well have something to eat. That's the spirit, I thought. Let's eat!

But what?

Then she pulled from her carry-on an enormous bag of walnuts. "Have some," she said, opening the bag and passing them around. Like everyone else sitting at the table, I took a handful and thanked her. It seems this woman was from California, and naturally, she'd brought walnuts, although in hindsight she might just as easily have brought pistachios or the ubiquitous almond.

Regardless, I was grateful for the walnuts, and I learned that this woman, who was a health enthusiast and thin as a seedling, ate her share of them. The thought occurred to me that we were, at that moment, probably the only ones in Cuba eating walnuts.

The other day I did something I don't often do. I turned on the television. And before I could pick up the clicker to click my way over to my local PBS station for the *PBS News Hour* or *Nova* or *Doc Martin*, or whatever was on, I was treated to a commercial for, not Cuban cigars or rum, but "heart-healthy California walnuts." This was certainly a surprise. Did the walnut industry somehow sense pecans nipping at its heels? This is doubtful. According to the agricultural marketers I've spoken to, walnuts have nothing to fear from America's indigenous tree nut. And that's because, despite what many consider to be the pecan's inimitable flavor, and in spite of research showing the pecan's super-rich oil content and antioxidant levels, pecans, though they've been here on the North American continent much longer than we have, have an image problem.

This is due to many factors, including the pecan industry's traditionally fragmented structure. Unlike America's walnut or almond industries—which are concentrated in California, where growers share common environmental challenges and concerns—the pecan belt includes fifteen states spread out across the southern United States, from the Pacific to the Atlantic. The challenges that pecan farmers in Arizona or New Mexico face are very different from those in Alabama or Mississippi or South Carolina. And this is to say nothing of the long-standing rivalries between various stakeholder groups, such as growers and shellers, groups that even today may work against one another, affecting prices and skewing related data.

It also reflects the pecan's provincial image as a food item closely associated with the American South, as well as the public's traditional view of the pecan as a holiday staple, one synonymous with sweet treats like pies and cookies.

At the kickoff meeting to a recent leadership workshop in Utah, one of the staff came out on stage and told the audience that her job was essentially that of a valet, that if an attendee needed anything at all, she would locate the item and get it to them. She also stated that in all the years she'd been doing this, there had been only one item she'd failed to provide. It seems that some years earlier a man from England was attending the workshop and somehow he'd heard about America's blue-ribbon tree nut. He wanted to try roasted pecans. The valet searched all the grocery stores and specialty markets in the area, but the only pecans she could locate were a bag of raw pieces on the baking aisle at a local supermarket. Fortunately, this is changing.

Additionally, and maybe most importantly, pecans as a generic product have traditionally had no domestic promotion. As a result, many Americans know relatively little about their country's indigenous tree nut, which is, incidentally, one of its most important native crops. This fact is quite apparent when talking with people from other parts of the world, such as Asia, who often know more about our homegrown nut than we do. They know that pecans are brimming with heart-healthy oils and packed with vitamins, minerals, and antioxidants, for example. Ask an American, and you're likely to hear about how Grandma uses pecans for baking pies at Thanksgiving or how someone else likes pecans in their ice cream. Some may tell you pecans are getting too expensive and that they're opting instead for less expensive walnuts or almonds. Regrettably, many US citizens know nothing about pecans because they've never seen one, never tasted one.

Alex Willson, chief operating officer at Sunnyland Farms, in Albany, Georgia, told of representing his company at the International Restaurant and Foodservice Show of New York, where he introduced visitors to pecans, many for the first time. "Some visitors would come up, and they didn't know anything about pecans," Willson told me.

Many Europeans certainly do, including some who recognize the pecan's succulent flavor as its supreme asset. On a recent visit to Italy, my host, a well-known Tuscan chef, inquired about my current writing projects. When I mentioned the word "pecans," she perked up and said that she loves these nuts and prefers them to all others for certain recipes. Then she added that she is seldom able to use them because she can almost never find pecans in her local shops or markets.

Chinese consumers, on the other hand, seem to have no trouble finding pecans, something they know as a luxury item, a food enjoyed for holidays and celebrations for those who can afford them. Indeed, in many parts of the world, consumers are quick to point out the high prices they must pay to enjoy pecans. Someone from Chile recently remarked that in his country, a small, snack-pack-sized package of pecans cost the equivalent of thirty US dollars. Obviously, at these prices pecans aren't going to be seen as the people's nut. Perhaps the prince's preferred nut is more like it. But price is only one obstacle. The real challenge for many consumers is understanding the specific value the pecan represents. Ironically, this might be most problematic here at home, where we have virtually unlimited access to so many different varieties of tree nuts and yet a population that understands relatively little about them. While this challenge isn't limited to pecans, developing a clear and consistent brand is vital to this industry's future success, especially considering that pecans are typically some of and often the highest-priced nuts on store shelves.

As someone who has conceptualized and created more than a few marketing and advertising campaigns, it seems to me—and this is only my opinion—that the US pecan industry can do a better job of differentiating its product from competitors. It also needs to identify a target (ideal) consumer. Determine what this nut provides better than any other product in the world and identify who needs it. Then figure out how to match the two.

Currently, pecans are competing in what business consultants often refer to as a "red sea," in which rival companies are continually trying to undercut or even devour one another. This is a setting in which the pecan industry is ill-equipped to win. The sheer volume of almonds and walnuts produced each year all but guarantees this. What the industry might do is figure out how to get to that proverbial "blue sea," where due to the pecan's competitive advantage, competition is greatly reduced. To get here the industry must decide if its product is going to be seen as the quintessential baking ingredient, nature's preventive medicine, a supremely tasty snack for people on the go, or simply the patriotic tree nut, America's own pecan. Or maybe it's something else. Again, what does the pecan provide better than any other product in the world? While it might be all of these to some extent, it must be one of these above all else. Consumers, particularly American consumers, many of whom already associate pecans with high-calorie pies and other goodies, want to know which one it is. And the pecan industry has but a few seconds to reach us and deliver its message. Though we're hungry, and though we clamor for nutritious foods, and though we have access to endless information to help inform our decisions, as a society we are distracted more than ever. The challenge is to have the brand so well associated with the image of a pecan that, once viewed, the consumer makes this connection almost instantly. This is tough to do, especially when presenting a diverse value proposition. By simplifying, however, by reinforcing one supreme value above all others—the pecan's unique flavor, for instance—the industry could greatly clarify and enhance its brand.

Some industry leaders have pointed out that they view their product, the pecan, as a premium item that warrants a premium price. That's fine. But premium on what basis? Oil content? Health benefits? Convenience? And premium for whom?

Perhaps recognizing the potential for increased brand recognition and value, growers across the US pecan belt have planted thousands of acres of new trees in recent years. Just how many acres or trees is difficult to say. That's because some of these plantings are not actually new, but replacements. Many growers are removing existing trees and replacing them with varieties such as Desirable and Pawnee, which produce the massive, well-filled pecans that Chinese buyers demand. As a result of all these new and replacement plantings, the industry is expecting millions of pounds of surplus product in the coming years. This presents one of the primary challenges, and opportunities, for the US pecan industry—increasing demand for its product.

Hilton Segler, executive director of the National Pecan Growers Council, told me in a 2016 interview that the industry is seeking to expand upon the recent marketing efforts that have made its product such a hit internationally. Its target now is the domestic market.

"What the next decade brings will depend on the success of research funds that we put into the nutritional and health benefits to consumers," Segler said. "It will depend on our production and promotion, and on the success of our national marketing program of promoting pecans domestically. This is where the real market is, more so than internationally. We feel that with pecans, with their health benefits, we can accomplish the same thing here domestically that we have introduced to the international trade. We're looking for a bright future," he said.

Rain. More rain. More rain for southern Oklahoma. Rain. Filling the Washita River. Filling the Red River. Swollen rivers swelling Cumberland Pool, flooding the Tishomingo National Wildlife Refuge, brown water backing up, up, creeping across low-lying fields and forests, high water rising, swamping the champion pecan, swamping the grove of ancients with which it keeps watch over the vast field of green, sweeping a new blanket of sediment onto the alluvial floodplain, washing away my idea for a visit today to Oklahoma's greatest pecan tree.

—5—

Sheller's Market

The day following my interview with Brett Mason, he calls to tell me he's just received a small order of pecans for shelling and invites me to observe the process.

As I enter the store Maran comes out to greet me, chipper as always, and I talk with her for several minutes about the importance of art in our schools. Brett appears, and we head into the processing room. Custom shelling was how Mason's Pecans got its start, and Brett tells me that today, fifty years later, it's still an important part of the business.

"Most years about eighty percent of our profits come from shelling," he says. "That didn't happen last year because we had a very light crop, but most years that's how it is. The retail store accounts for the rest."

The order he just received consists of several brown paper grocery bags of Stuarts, one of the oldest pecan cultivars. Its resistance to scab—the most problematic fungal disease affecting pecans today—has declined over the years as the scab organism has evolved, and with so many newer and better varieties available, Stuart is beginning to fall from favor, especially for new plantings. These Stuarts didn't come from a commercial orchard, however, but from a woman with a few backyard trees.

With summer only a few weeks away, I ask Brett if it's not late in the year for customers to be bringing him pecans for shelling. He admits that it is and tells me that October through February is the busy season. Perhaps this explains why he doesn't seem particularly excited about this order of pecans. How fresh can they be if they've lain on the ground or sat in someone's garage for months? He cracks one and examines the kernel. It looks fine to my eyes. And the color seems perfect—a light golden color. Brett isn't impressed.

"The shell didn't fill out the way it should have," he says. "Stuarts are known for that. There's a void inside. It doesn't fill out and that causes a lot of the kernels to fragment during shelling."

"Sure, but that's still a nice-looking kernel, no?"

"I've seen a lot better," he says.

This order of nuts also includes many sticks, leaves, and poppers, a term Brett uses to describe pecans still encased in the hull and not fully developed. He fills a small plastic bag with several pieces of this debris and tells me he intends to include it with the customer's order as a reminder that he prefers to receive and crack only pecans rather than sticks and rocks and other items that tend to damage his expensive processing equipment. This equipment consists of six different machines lining one wall of the Mason's Pecans processing room, including a pair of crackers, an old shelling machine, a shaker table—an innocuous-looking contraption producing an inordinate amount of noise given that its primary function is to remove dust from the shells and kernels—and a two-stage separator.

Brett begins by dumping a bag of pecans into the cracking machine, a shiny, new stainless-steel contraption featuring a panel of gauges, knobs, oilers, valves, hoses, and an electric control panel, which makes it look like something out of a 1950s science-fiction film.

But it's not fiction. It's the pecan industry's state-of-the-art cracking machine, produced by the Savage equipment company of Madill, Oklahoma.

Brett tells me there are not as many custom shellers as there used to be. However, heavy-crop years tend to entice at least a few more to jump into the business to try to make a go of it, regardless of whether they know anything about pecan processing, trees, or the nuts themselves.

"There was one guy who opened up a shop in Oklahoma City a few years ago after a heavy crop the previous season," Brett tells me. "He rented a building, and instead of investing in good equipment, he bought cheap stuff. He didn't know what he was doing, and his business didn't last long. He came to work for me to see what he was doing wrong. He told me later that we did it differently than how he'd done it. I said we've been shelling pecans a long time. This is what we do."

Mason's Pecans is known for its quality shelling. In fact, the pecans Brett is processing today came from a woman in Guthrie, Oklahoma's original state capital, an hour away. She'd made the drive to Mason's because, as she said, her local sheller didn't do as good a job.

What's Brett's secret? Experience, skill, and the best equipment.

This equipment begins with the pair of Savage cracking machines. They're air powered and chain driven, held together with nuts and bolts and welding beads smooth and neat. The pecans are dumped into the feeding chute on top, where they find their way onto a conveyor belt apparatus that carries them, one by one, into the cracker. A blast of air cracks the shell. The cracked pecans are then released into a bucket beneath the machine.

These air blasts are quite powerful, and they can be adjusted for shell density. Native pecans, or those with thicker shells, require more force to crack than, say, a papershell variety. For this reason the user must tailor the cracking pressure to the specific variety of pecan being processed in order to protect the valuable kernels from damage.

Opening up the protective hood covering the cracking apparatus reveals a stainless-steel manifold with "SAVAGE: MADILL, OKLAHOMA" engraved on its face and several air hoses feeding into each pecan-holding chamber. Brett says when he was a kid, back in the sixties, his father, Bill, took him to the Savage plant in Madill, where its namesake owner and innovator, Basil Savage, had a prototype for this very cracking machine.

"I remember it being very big," Brett says. "It was a big machine. When I came back to Oklahoma and took over the business in 2005, I was surprised how much smaller and more manageable the final product turned out to be."

To hear Brett and nearly every other sheller I've spoken to throughout the pecan belt talk of the Savage pecan-cracking machine is like listening to someone describe a new pickup truck just purchased after driving around in an old jalopy for the past decade or more.

"The old-style machines would crack about sixty nuts an hour," Brett says. "The Savage will crack four hundred an hour, and it does a better job."

As with the cracking pressure, the machine's speed can be adjusted to suit conditions or user preferences, and in full swing the unit sounds like something reminiscent of low-velocity machine-gun fire. Lowering the speed to somewhere between 250 and 300 nuts per minute, one is treated to the clicking-clacking clatter of an Abrams tank tracking across a battlefield.

Lifting the protective hood to expose the cracking apparatus stops the machine—an obvious safety feature—but in overriding it, one is able to witness the cracker's power. Donning a protective mask and cover, I move up to the front lines of the action where with each rifle-like crack the machine sends out a blast of splintered organic shrapnel.

Which, as far as I can see, is all the more reason for the cracking machine's heavy-duty construction. The stainless-steel sheets are strong, and they provide a measure of protection against the exploding pecan shells inside. But Brett tells me it's also another way of upping the ante in the war of attrition.

"Commercial shellers are required to use stainless-steel processing machines, rather than those made of lower-cost aluminum," he says. "Custom shellers don't have this requirement. Yet. But we will. It's happened in other nut industries, and it'll happen with pecans. It's just another way for the big guys to stick it to the little guys. These cracking machines cost almost fifteen thousand dollars apiece. If we're required to have stainless-steel equipment, a lot of smaller processors won't be able to afford it. It's a way of creating a monopoly."

The cracked pecans then go to the shelling machine, which tumbles the nuts to further loosen the shells. Brett says the new crackers, like the Savage machines, work so well they make shellers almost obsolete, although he concedes there is still some benefit in using them. His is a Meyer sheller, made in San Antonio, Texas, in the early 1980s. It features an air-blowing precleaner that removes excess debris from the pecans. This feature is proving invaluable today, although if Brett is frustrated, he doesn't show it. Sticks and stones may require an extra step or two, but they're not as troublesome as the nails, screws, and even bolts that show up in pecan orders from time to time.

"If we get those, I just call the customer and tell them we can't process the order," he says. "We shell pecans, not screws or bolts."

The sheller looks old-fashioned compared to the shiny Savage cracking machines beside it, yet it performs admirably. Before shelling, Brett actually takes one of the newly cracked pecan kernels and uses this as a gauge as he adjusts the discs inside the machine. This ensures that anything larger than the kernel is treated and processed as it passes through, with the result that more shells are removed from kernels.

Swinging the bucket of semi-shelled pecan kernels and shell fragments onto the next station with the familiarity of a basketball player laying the ball into the hoop, Brett next activates the shaker table. This simple-looking machine feeds the nuts onto a sheet of quarter-inch hardware cloth, which is then shaken back and forth for the purpose of removing dust from the product. It is very noisy, even compared to the other machines.

From here, Brett takes the bucket of shaken nuts and slam dunks them into the separator, which features a two-stage blower to separate, once and for all, kernels from shells. This machine, too, is a Meyer, produced in San Antonio. Kernel halves, pieces, and separated shells are fed into three chutes and ultimately bagged. Shells are sold as mulch. The pecan kernels are labeled with the claim ticket, which accompanies the order through the entire process so as to ensure the customer gets his or her pecans and not those from another batch.

Brett says women do a better job folding and labeling the brown paper bags containing the pecan "meats," but he stresses to all his employees the importance of being professional and delivering quality work. This would require, for me at least, wearing ear protection. The processing machines are all quite strident, particularly the shaker table, and especially when they're all running simultaneously.

Yields (the percentage of kernels or meats resulting from each pound of processed pecans) range from around 30 percent for natives, given their typically heavier, denser shells, to roughly 50 percent for cultivars such as Elliott.

Brett says he can process 400 pounds of pecans per hour, and 2,000 pounds over an eight-hour shift. This is less a reflection of his equipment's capability, perhaps, than it is an indicator of Brett's experience and skill, which permit him to get the most out of his processing machines. Speed, tension, pressure: these are just some of the variables that must be manipulated with each batch of pecans fed into the cracking machine. Once this is operating smoothly, a skilled processor can then move to the next station, and the next, until all the machines are operating simultaneously and the pecans moving continuously through the cracking and shelling continuum. Ideally, as one cohort of pecans is cycling through the cracker, another is completing the shelling process, while another is spilling out of the separator and into brown paper bags to await customer pickup. A neophyte sheller might simply feed pecans into each machine, stand back and await the results, but a highly skilled processor like Brett manipulates each machine to produce exactly the results he wishes, at the speed he desires, permitting him to make the most efficient use of his time. There is simply so much more to pecan processing, even small-scale custom shelling, than meets the eye, and this is my first significant takeaway from today's experience.

As Brett places a newly shelled bag of kernels onto a wire rack, I notice several other brown paper sacks on the shelf, waiting to be claimed. This sight produces today's second major takeaway: the bottom half of each—that portion of the bag actually in contact with the kernels—is solidly dark from the absorbed pecan oil, that succulent product that gives these nuts their flavor and salubrious reputation. I don't mean to suggest these bags were merely discolored or a bit oily. They were *soaked* in oil!

We leave the processing room and move back into the Mason's Pecans store. As the door closes behind us, as I begin to regain my sense of hearing, Brett shows me the written log of orders awaiting customer pickup.

"Some of our older customers want their pecans cracked but not shelled," he tells me. "They eat them at night while they sit and watch television, and they like to shell them themselves. My mother always believed that eating a few pecans every day was a smart thing to do, especially for people with arthritis. Not only is the oil good for you, but the motion of using your fingers to shell pecans helps keep them nimble. It's like exercise for your fingers."

Cracked pecans make a simple and savory snack while allowing us the tactile pleasure of shelling the kernels ourselves.

Despite the continued popularity and profitability of improved varieties after more than a century of diligent cultivation, natives continue to figure strongly into the annual production of several traditional pecan-producing states. According to the US Department of Agriculture (USDA), native and seedling pecans accounted for nearly 20 percent (twelve million pounds) of the 2014 Texas harvest, and in Louisiana 82 percent of its annual harvest for this same year consisted of natives. The USDA reports that native and seedlings accounted for two-thirds (66 percent) of Oklahoma's 2014 harvest, and this was at a time of severe drought for the state. Just one year earlier, natives dominated Oklahoma's annual harvest, accounting for 85 percent of total pecan production.

A Louisiana pecan farmer told me that many landowners in his area consider native pecans an incidental, but welcome, supplement to other crops or livestock. He said they go well with cattle because the trees provide shade without requiring much maintenance from the landowner. And the cattle, he said, provide the fertilizer.

While China's seemingly insatiable demand for the pecan has reinvigorated the industry, giving growers a reason to be optimistic about the future, it wants large, thin-shelled nuts, the kind produced by cultivated trees. Nuts this size may run forty or so to a pound. Natives are smaller, often much smaller, with shells that are typically tougher to crack. Processing these smaller, thick-shelled pecans can result in a large percentage of broken kernels. Perhaps surprisingly, however, current wholesale rates for pecan halves and pieces are very similar. As of this writing (2016), most pieces are trading between \$6.35 and \$6.55 a pound, "freight on board," a term reflecting the actual cost of the nuts themselves plus, for the buyer, the additional expenses of trucking and insurance. With freight on board (FOB), the buyer assumes ownership of the product from the moment it's loaded onto the truck at the seller's facility.

Likewise, most pecan halves are trading between $6.40 and $6.75 a pound, FOB.

To some extent the Patrick refutes the smaller-but-thicker stereotype, however, as it's a diminutive, native pecan that's also easy to crack. But in a market that demands the largest pecans, it may not be economically viable, even though native pecans are often said to have a higher oil content and superior flavor compared to their domesticated counterparts.

Despite their current limited commercial value, and in spite of the movement away from wild trees toward high-yielding cultivars, the pecan industry is working to find new markets for native pecans, which are very much an underutilized resource. To that end, the new federal marketing order (FMO) is providing funding to support the organized promotion of pecans, such as that which has long been done for other tree-nut crops, like almonds. The seventeen-member American Pecan Council administers the FMO and coordinates pecan-related research, establishes quality standards, and otherwise works to increase demand for the nut. While much of the FMO centers on the expected increase in annual pecan production as a result of significant new acreage being planted in the United States over the past five years, the possibility of finding new markets for native pecans is cause for optimism.

Cindy Wise of the Texas Pecan Growers Association told me in 2016 that often the price for native pecans is too low for growers to invest the money in actually harvesting them. This contributes to the devaluing of wild pecan trees, and it has driven some landowners to replace groves of these native trees with cultivars capable of producing bumper crops of mammoth-sized pecans. Ms. Wise told me that new markets for native pecans would increase demand, which should improve prices. If the harvesting of these smaller pecans proves profitable, this could enhance the value of native trees and give landowners a greater incentive to manage and protect them.

Months later, on a sunny, crisp, fall morning, the day before Thanksgiving, in fact, I exit Interstate 40 and drive south toward Valley View Pecan Company, just east of Shawnee, Oklahoma. The road must have been recently paved because it's the smoothest Oklahoma thoroughfare I've driven on in quite some time. Cattle graze beneath pecan trees in the surrounding, gently rolling fields to the east and west.

Inside the Valley View store the shelves are stocked with bags of Pawnee pecan halves. Pecan pralines are stacked near the cash register. Behind the cash register is Janice Grundmann, the proprietor, who smiles when I introduce myself and ask if I can tour her company's processing room. Janice thinks it over for a moment and then tells me she normally doesn't allow this because in the past those who've toured the back room have almost invariably, and inexplicably, thrust their hands into the barrels of pecan halves. When I promise to not touch anything, Janice says she'll make an exception. She then disappears into the back room to get her son Josh Grundmann, who manages the commercial processing.

Josh is thirtyish with dark hair and the kind of easy grin that says he enjoys his work. His father, John Grundmann, started in custom shelling in 1973 and entered commercial processing about thirty years later. Josh studied agriculture engineering at Oklahoma State University and has been involved in the family business for nine years. During the busy season, which is now, he gets one day off each week to watch football on Saturday. Beyond this, however, he stays busy managing a shelling operation that employs nine people and processes between 200,000 and 300,000 pounds of pecans each season.

As a commercial shelling company, Valley View's processing room resembles others I've visited, only the machines here are larger and more numerous. This morning Josh is processing an order of Kanza pecans—what he calls Oklahoma's silver-medal variety. He says Pawnee—the large ones out on the store shelves—get the gold medal. We stop in front of a cracking machine. It's a Savage, like the one Brett

Mason uses, only larger and capable of cracking pecans at a higher rate of speed, currently 700 nuts per minute. I peer into the bin on top and see the Kanzas funneling through. Their shells are light in color with almost none of the dark streaks that mark those of other varieties. When I comment to Josh that his processing room is surprisingly dust free, he laughs and mentions the aspirator pipe system that, along with the cracker, produces a constant droning noise requiring us to elevate our voices to communicate. The pipes are connected to a large blower that produces a low air pressure. Evidently, this blower moves a lot of air, which causes lighter particles (shells and dust) to be pulled away from the pecans and isolated while the heavier particles (kernels) fall from the aspirator and are collected in large buckets. The shells, sold as mulch, are gathered separately. A large auger feeds these shells into a grain bin outside. Judging by the lack of dust inside the processing room, the aspirator pipe system is remarkably effective and is one of the most impressive aspects of Valley View's shelling operation.

One of the things that differentiates commercial shelling from custom shelling is the quantity of pecans each processes. Josh says that as a commercial sheller he doesn't shell ten-pound orders, but rather orders of five hundred pounds, minimum. His father continues to do some custom shelling in a separate facility, where he can handle small-scale orders.

Also, unlike custom shellers who process pecans for hobby and backyard growers, Valley View's customers are mostly commercial growers from all around Oklahoma.

Another thing that separates commercial shellers from most small operations is the emphasis they place on sanitizing pecans before processing. Josh points out a large vat containing 1,500 gallons of water, which he's in the process of heating to 180 degrees—not quite a boil, he says, but a simmer. Into this he will immerse the heavy, square cage sitting on the floor nearby, which contains 500 pounds of pecans. He submerges the pecans in the hot water for five minutes, which neutralizes E. coli or any other bacteria the shells may harbor as a result of lying on the ground in a cattle pasture, where many pecans are harvested.

The other major difference is that pecans processed by a commercial sheller do not contain the shell fragments you get occasionally in orders processed by smaller shellers. They take the pecans through the extra steps necessary to remove these fragments. One of these extra steps, which I've not seen elsewhere, is performed by what Josh calls the "eye machine," a lofty piece of equipment containing two cameras designed to inspect pecan kernels for color, allowing the lighter-color kernels to pass through while rejecting those dark or off-colored pieces. It's a Satake optical sorting machine, produced by Satake USA, Inc., of Stafford, Texas, a wholly owned subsidiary of the Satake Corporation of Japan, whose Vision Systems operation designs, manufactures, and services sophisticated optical sorters for a range of food products, with equipment featuring fully digital image processing, shape recognition, enhanced 3-D sorting programs, LED illumination, and high-resolution full-color cameras. Josh says the machine greatly simplifies and accelerates the task of separating errant pecan halves. Indeed, when he turns the machine on, kernels begin spilling out of a funnel and into a large barrel. As I glance into the barrel, I realize the kernels are of a uniform size and color.

When I comment that this sure beats inspecting kernels by hand, Josh says that is what happens at the next station. He then leads me into a room where two women are sitting along a buzzing conveyor belt rapidly finessing the pecan halves speeding past them. These are larger halves, Pawnees. The women catch anything the "eye machine" misses. Then they package these halves into thirty-pound cases, tape the boxes shut, and stack them on nearby pallets for customer pickup.

After my tour we go back into the store, and I buy a bag of native pecans. With Thanksgiving tomorrow, desserts must be on everyone's mind. Josh comments that these natives are perfect for pecan pie. I tell him I just like to snack on them.

"They're perfect for eating plain because they have more oil and taste better than others," he says.

On the way out the door, I wish the Grundmanns a happy Thanksgiving. Josh grins. "I might take the day off," he says.

—6—

Big Oil

After hearing so much about the benefits of native pecans specifically and listening to pecan men and women sing the praises of these wild nuts, lauding them for their rich oil and superior flavor, I made it a point to pick up a bag on my last visit to Mason's Pecans. With their high oil content, pecans quickly turn rancid when stored at room temperature. For this reason I'm told it's better to refrigerate them, and freezing pecans preserves their freshness even longer.

As I didn't know when I might bust into my new bag of natives, I placed them in the freezer and forgot about them. Then, one day when my supply of roasted, salted pecans ran low, I looked in the freezer. There was a sticky note on the bag. "Do Not Open," it read.

Who was claiming my pecans?

As it turns out, my wife was. She was headed to a business seminar in the mountain West and told me that she'd been asked to bring something from home, something that represented Oklahoma. Pecans, native pecans, were just the thing, she said. I agreed with her, but did it have to be my native pecans?

At the seminar she met a woman from Shanghai, who raved about these nuts. We eat them in China, the woman told my wife. I know people who grow them in their yards, she said. We eat them for holidays. We love pecans because they're so good for us. It's the oil, she said. We eat lots of different nuts, but we love pecans because we feel they're a good value for our children. (She used the word "value.") The oil in pecans will make our children smart.

Somewhere I'd heard this before. It's almost as if we can't talk about pecans without mentioning their oil content. Indeed, my *Britannica World Language Dictionary* includes, in its definition of the pecan, a reference to this oil: "The nut borne by this tree, containing a sweet, oily kernel."

There is no mention whatsoever of oil or oily kernels in the dictionary's listings for almonds, hazelnuts, pistachios, walnuts, or any other nut I've looked up. It seems when it comes to oil, at least as it pertains to nuts, pecans are in a class by themselves. Thinking about it reminds me of the day I observed Brett Mason processing an order of these nuts for a customer and saw several oil-soaked bags of shelled pecans awaiting pickup. It's one thing to use a precision screw press to force out every last drop of oil from the nuts; it's quite another to see this oil slowly, steadily ooze from the fresh kernels and soak into the brown paper. Though I've been studying pecans for only a few years, the people I've met in researching this book are the world's experts on them. And I would venture to say the very essence of what they do, and what I'm doing in writing this book, goes back to that oil oozing from those shelled kernels, giving pecans their inimitable flavor and providing those who eat them with a seemingly endless array of health benefits.

"We used to eat only walnuts, and then we saw on TV that pecans are more nutritious than walnuts," one Chinese woman told a reporter. "Pecans are very good for the brain," she said. "We older people should eat more pecans so that we don't get Alzheimer's."

Or cancer.

Dr. Luis Cisneros-Zevallos, a professor of food science and nutrition at Texas A&M University, is nearing the final phase of a long-term study into the pecan's anti-inflammatory properties. His research has shown that pecans reduce inflammation in cells and decrease fat accumulation in fat cells, which he says makes them a potent dietary tool for the prevention of diseases such as cancer. There is also evidence suggesting pecans are beneficial for colon health, as the natural chemicals in these nuts metabolize microorganisms in the gut. Dr. Cisneros-Zevallos is now looking at how the chemical compounds in pecans may affect other diseases.

The medicinal value of pecans is something we've understood for a long time. Louisiana Creole culture includes a number of traditional remedies for diarrhea, for example, including a tea made with an infusion of pecan husks, bark, and leaves steeped in whiskey. This was once a popular tonic and evidently quite effective due to what some believed was the pecan's astringent quality and its high levels of tannins. Similarly, the Cajuns used a solution made from boiled pecan leaves and a dash of "cooking soda" as a treatment for athlete's foot.

Today, however, we understand more about what pecans can aid in preventing.

"When people consume these nuts, they're consuming a product loaded with beneficial chemical compounds," Cisneros-Zevallos told me during a 2016 interview. "Pecans are very rich compared to other nuts. All nuts are good, but pecans apparently have more of these beneficial compounds."

They're also packed with thiamine, magnesium, calcium, folic acid, potassium, and zinc, while containing cholesterol-lowering omega-6 and omega-3 fatty acids. Pecan oil contains surprisingly high levels of oleic acid—the same heart-healthy monounsaturated fatty acid found in olives—which has the ability to suppress a gene thought to trigger breast cancer. Laboratory studies have revealed that the form of vitamin E found in pecans, gamma-tocopherol, has been shown to inhibit prostate cancer cells while ignoring healthy tissues. Additionally, there is evidence that the high level of antioxidants in pecans may help protect the nervous system and delay the progression of such degenerative conditions as Alzheimer's disease or amyotrophic lateral sclerosis (ALS).

In the *Encyclopedia of Healing Foods* (2005), author and researcher Michael Murray, ND, writes that pecans owe much of their flavor to their high fat content, most of which is in the form of heart-healthy monounsaturated oleic acid. He notes that a one-ounce (one-quarter cup) serving of pecans provides 190 calories, nearly 20 grams of fat (46 percent of which is monounsaturated), 2.6 grams of protein, almost 4 grams of carbohydrate, and 2.72 grams of fiber.

The American Heart Association recommends four to five servings of nuts, seeds, or legumes each week as part of a balanced diet. While some may be reluctant to make pecans a regular part of their diet, given the nut's high caloric content, Murray points to studies showing that the healthy fats in pecans do not lead to unhealthy excess fat stores in humans. He also says that the generous macro- and micronutrient content of pecans justifies their high calorie count. For optimal nutrition the Mayo Clinic suggests raw or dry-roasted nuts rather than those cooked in oil and adds that pecans make an excellent substitute for the saturated fats found in eggs, meat, and dairy products.

Murray says that, in addition to their generous monounsaturated fat content, pecans also contain high levels of plant sterols, which have been widely researched for their ability to reduce cholesterol. "By competing with cholesterol for absorption from the intestine," he writes, "beta-sitosterol and other plant sterols have been shown to lower LDL (bad) cholesterol concentrations by 10 to 14 percent." To support this claim, Murray cites studies conducted at New Mexico State University and at Loma Linda University in which daily pecan consumption significantly lowered LDL cholesterol in research participants.

According to Murray, a one-ounce serving of pecans can contain up to 27 milligrams of these plant sterols, including as much as 24

Not just for Thanksgiving anymore, pecans are a legitimate superfood whose inimitable flavor elevates snacks and meals into something special.

percent beta-sitosterol. If this isn't enough, he adds that pecans are an excellent source of vitamins B1, B3, B5, and B6, among others.

Researchers James L. Hargrove, PhD, Diane K. Hartle, PhD, and Phillip Greenspan, PhD, point out in their book, *Health Benefits of Pecans* (2013), that pecans contain the most antioxidant, phenolic compounds among nuts, and more flavonoids than other common nuts. The researchers also rank the antioxidant activity of pecans among the highest of all common US foods, higher even than such noted superfoods as blueberries and raspberries.

It seems that eating pecans may be one of the smartest things we can do. American Indians realized this thousands of years ago. The Chinese understand, even though they were introduced to these nuts only a few years ago. Slowly, American consumers are realizing that pecans can be tremendous assets in maintaining health and preventing disease. Indeed, this is the trend in medicine today. Doctors and researchers strive to empower patients to become active participants in their own health care. Medical providers deliver the acute and reactive treatments. They take care of us when we're sick. But it's those daily lifestyle choices we make that have such a significant impact on our overall and long-term health that really matter, and each of us has the power to decide how we're going to live and care for ourselves day to day. Pecans, with their high levels of antioxidants and numerous other health benefits, can play an important role in this.

Stress and disorders can lead to high levels of free radicals in the body. These are reactive molecules that contribute to tissue damage. When free radicals increase, they may induce inflammation, which Dr. Cisneros-Zevallos calls "the mother of all big problems you will encounter in diseases, like diabetes, cancer, and Alzheimer's." Consuming antioxidants, then, such as those provided by pecans, can reduce levels of these free radicals, and in doing so, reduce inflammation, helping to prevent diseases. Dr. Cisneros-Zevallos and his team are now trying to understand how the chemical compounds in pecans—specifically, polyphenols, those antioxidant-rich phytochemicals believed to protect against some health problems and the effects of aging—may affect diabetes. This is needed today more than ever.

"Here in the US, something happened in our society in the 1950s, and we didn't recover," he said. "We began eating all this junk food. We didn't eat right. This is being reflected today in society's obesity trends, and in the number of cases of metabolic syndrome. But if we give people the right tools, guide them to pay attention to the right crops, I believe we can reverse these things. It can take one or two generations, but we can reduce those numbers and restore our health. I believe that pecans will help us do this."

One New Mexico grower told me recently that in China pecans are known as brain food. Eating them is good for mental health, he said. But it's also visual. When you take a pecan kernel out of the shell, it has these deep grooves in it. They say it looks like a human brain.

Recently I've been hearing a great deal about the benefits of pecan oil. Having never cooked with it, having never tasted this oil beyond eating pecans themselves, I decide to see what all the excitement is about. So I visit my local Whole Foods supermarket. With its extensive and diverse selection of cooking oils, I reason that I'm more likely to find pecan oil here than anywhere else in Oklahoma City. But I'm wrong. What I find instead are shelves of the ubiquitous olive oil in both virgin and extra-virgin varieties and in varying quantities from various manufacturers. Also, I find palm oil. And coconut oil, which sounds fun, but I'm looking specifically for pecan oil, so I continue my search. I find oils made from sunflower, avocado, and, surprisingly, pistachio nuts.

There are even three varieties of almond oil, and there's walnut oil, lovingly bottled, smartly labeled, prominently displayed, but no pecan oil in any quantity from any manufacturer occupying any shelf space whatsoever.

I'm surprised at the lack of pecan oil. This is the pecan belt, after all. And this is a supermarket chain founded in Austin, Texas, which might be the buckle of that belt. Where's the pecan oil?

I send the question off in an e-mail message to Whole Foods management. The next day, while waiting for a response, I climb behind the wheel of my wholly "unnew" Toyota automobile and point its hood south, toward Coleman, Oklahoma, a tiny farming community with only one traffic light, a co-op, a couple of gas stations, and a public-school system. Getting there is half the fun, however, and that's because I have to drive through some very rural, very remote, very picturesque countryside, which, for someone who doesn't get out of the city as often as he'd like, is invigorating and wholly liberating. It's as fine a summer day as there ever was, or ever will be, probably. Brilliant sunshine filters down from the sky, illuminating the expansive fields, which are lush and green and teeming with colorful sheens of wildflowers. Scissor-tailed flycatchers flutter over these fields, catching insects, scissoring the air with their long, slender tails, and alighting on barbed-wire fences and power lines as they watch me drive by. Deer bound through meadows and across the country road in front of me, slipping beneath these same barbed-wire fences. And as I cross a bridge spanning the Blue River, in Johnston County, I delight in the sight of its cool waters spilling over small waterfalls and into clear pools.

Coleman is in that part of the state where the rolling hills begin to grow in size and where stands of pine trees appear from time to time. It's like a gateway into southeastern Oklahoma, the Choctaw Nation.

At the Tri-Agri Farm Center, just across from the Coleman Public Schools, I find Mark Hamilton slurping coffee from a mug. He's dressed in blue jeans, a short-sleeved polo-style shirt, and a red cap. Mark, whose family is Choctaw, is a retired math and computer-science teacher and baseball coach. He describes himself as a country boy, and he's got the rural landscape and workingman's hands to prove it. He stands about five feet ten inches with a wiry frame, sandy hair and mustache, and the muscular forearms of a hay hauler or cleanup hitter.

"You must've got up early this morning," he says in his relaxed Oklahoma drawl.

"I left the house at five thirty," I tell him, feeling at ease here in this small community.

It's now eight thirty, and a few farmers are milling around the Tri-Agri Farm Center store, buying feed, studying the labels on jugs of hydraulic fluid and oil and insecticides, trying on Wells-Lamont leather gloves, and talking and laughing and probably feeling happy because it's Friday. Though the store is humming with activity and percolating with the aroma of Folgers coffee dripping from the dripper in back, the parking lot outside is sleeping away the morning beneath a patchwork quilt of pickup trucks. Across the street a tired-looking warehouse and grain elevator appear to be enjoying the off-season.

Mark's father, Dan Hamilton, established the Tri-Agri Farm Center almost forty years ago. The business had its start in peanut processing before the Hamiltons turned their attention to pecans. Today the family operates one of the largest pecan cleaning and marketing operations in Oklahoma.

As a side business the Hamiltons started Native American Specialty Products, whose first offering is pecan oil. Pecans, especially native pecans, are an important crop in Oklahoma, where they grow wild. These are exactly the nuts Mark uses to produce his Achukma pecan oil—named for a Choctaw word meaning pure, healthy, natural.

Mark admits the product isn't flying off the shelves, but he says that's because most people don't know about pecan oil.

"Consumer education and marketing are some of our biggest challenges," he says. "We have to spend fifteen minutes teaching a potential customer about the benefits of pecan oil. Once they understand this, the product sells itself."

"What do your customers find most surprising about pecan oil?" I ask.

"That it even exists," he says. "We go to trade shows and we've found that outside the pecan industry, few people know anything about it. Early on, people would buy a bottle and never open it. They thought it was a novelty. Then they started using it and they liked it. Now we're getting a lot of repeat customers."

Mark tells me pecan oil is gluten free, is lower in saturated fat than olive oil, and is loaded with heart-healthy unsaturated fats. Also, it has a 470-degree smoke point, which is higher than almost any other type of cooking oil.

"We gave pecan oil to chefs for testing," Mark says. "Chefs like to cook an egg when they test a new oil. That tells them what they need to know. What they found with pecan oil is that they couldn't burn the egg."

Pecan oil is low in saturated fat and features a high smoke point. With pecans surging in popularity around the world, demand for this artisan cooking oil is beginning to grow as well.

Thinking back to my college days, I could have used something like this.

"It's not cheap," he says, "but it's not unreasonable either. It's priced about the same as high-grade olive oil. But it goes further. You use only about one-third the amount of pecan oil to achieve the same result as olive oil."

Mark leads the way as we head out of the store and toward the building where he produces his Achukma pecan oil. Along the way we pass through a small warehouse where he points to a commercial-grade roaster he just acquired. It has a conveyor belt to carry the product—in this case, pecans—through a large vat, which he intends to fill with, yes, pecan oil.

"We just bought this from a man in Long Island, New York," he says. "He used it to make plantain chips, but he went out of business. We ended up getting a good deal on it. By this fall, I hope to be roasting four thousand pounds a day."

"You're going to roast pecans in pecan oil?" I ask.

"That's right," he says as he opens a giant bag of recently roasted nuts. "Go ahead and take a few," he says.

I grab several of the dark-brown kernels and pop them into my mouth. They're crunchy, but not hard. They're sweet, with just a subtle hint of spice. They're delicious. I'm impressed.

"A lot of people roast their pecans at a lower temperature for a longer time," Mark says. "We do just the opposite. Cook them at a very high temperature for a short time. It sears the pecan, like a french fry, so it's crunchy on the outside. We've got a catering company down in Louisiana already requesting them."

With the flavor of roasted pecans still fresh in my mouth, we move over to the machine Mark uses to make his pecan oil. It's smaller than I imagined. It looks something like a woodworker's lathe, featuring an elongated horizontal tube but with a funnel on top to accept the pecans and a hose on bottom through which the pressed oil is drained into a holding tank.

"This is a tapered screw press," he says. "Made in Germany. It took us a long time to find it, but it makes all the difference. I bet there's not another one like it."

Mark says most presses in the United States are made for foods with low oil content. Not so this pecan-squeezing machine.

"This press is designed for a high-oil-content product," he says. "Its tapered-screw design allows us to squeeze more oil from the nuts. It makes sixteen to eighteen gallons an hour, about a hundred and fifty gallons a day."

Unlike many other pecan oils produced today, Mark's pure virgin Achukma oil is cold-pressed and never heated or treated with chemicals, which he says would degrade it.

"To be considered cold-pressed," he says, "the press has to run at a hundred and twenty degrees or less. We run ours between ninety and ninety-five degrees. There's a magnet in the hopper to catch any tiny bits of metal that come in with the nuts. From there the pecans are pressed and the beautiful, golden-brown oil filtered and stored in a holding tank for bottling."

Mark uses native pecans from Oklahoma and Texas. One hundred pounds of these small but tasty pecans produce sixty-two pounds of oil, and some thirty pounds of pecan meal, which can be used in various dishes and in baking. Mark says currently there is more demand for this meal, which is often called pecan flour, than the oil itself. But he's working to change this. He has even promoted his pecan oil in China.

"There's great demand over there," he says, "but we're hampered by tariffs. If we sent oil to China, we'd be facing a 12 percent tariff on the oil and a 15 percent value-added tax. Plus, their currency is inflated by anywhere from 15 to 35 percent. That's cost prohibitive. By contrast, if we imported pecan oil from China, if they had any, they would have to pay a tariff of only one-half of 1 percent."

In the meantime Hamilton is trying to improve demand here at home, focusing on the health-conscious American as a target client. It's not easy, especially in a market dominated by olive oil, but for those in the South Central states of Arkansas, Louisiana, Oklahoma, and Texas, pecan oil produced from native nuts fits perfectly with today's increasing demand for nutritious, locally grown foods—one reason why specialty retailers across the pecan belt are now beginning to carry pecan oil. Not long after my visit to Coleman, Oklahoma, and learning about Mark Hamilton's Native American Specialty Products, Whole Foods management notified me that several of its stores in the Southwest region, including my local supermarket, are now carrying this unique and intriguing contribution to artisan cooking oils.

Is it better than olive oil? So far, I've used pecan oil to fry an egg, but I'm not sure of anything other than the fact that the egg, though unburned, had a slight nutty flavor. More testing is needed.

—7—

Better by Nature

Americans were slow to warm up to the concept of organic foods. That's partly because when we noticed them at all, many of us couldn't appreciate their value. Organics were more expensive than their conventionally produced counterparts. They were offered in limited quantities. And they weren't available to all Americans. When they were, we were often too busy to notice and too accustomed to buying conventionally produced foods to educate ourselves about them.

After World War II we began to rely on others to do many of the things we'd always done for ourselves, including preparing the foods we eat. While the concept of fast food really took off in America during the 1950s, the automat chains in our northern industrial cities had been feeding us for decades. Customers would enter these establishments and select premade foods displayed behind glass windows. Once a selection was made, customers slipped coins into a slot, twisted the knob and presto, the window opened, allowing access to the food. Workers in the kitchen would then replenish the vacant compartment with a new dish in an early form of the strategy that would come to be known as "sandbagging," which fast-food chains perfected decades later.

Growing up, I was like a lot of other kids in 1970s America. Fast food, particularly McDonald's, was seen as a treat, as a reward for good grades or staying out of trouble. No matter how much of it my friends and I ate, we always wanted more. Had someone asked me to explain to them the concept of fast food, I very well may have described it like this: *Look, it's simple. There's McDonald's, and there's a whole bunch of other joints. But don't worry about them. Just remember McDonald's. Look for those golden arches and get in line.*

But it wasn't just the golden arches. Even more than this ubiquitous logo, it was the chain's red-and-yellow color scheme. As child psychologists knew, there was something exciting about this pairing, something that stirred the appetite within, probably because of the aroma of sizzling french fries that accompanied the sight of it.

I still remember the day my Cub Scout den visited McDonald's for an after-school field trip. We filed into the kitchen as the manager explained what was happening at each station:

This is the fry station. This is where we cook those french fries you enjoy so much. See that light? When it comes on that means the oil is hot enough. That's when we drop the fries.

"Look!" I said to a friend. "That's where the fries come from! Think they'll give us some?"

I don't think so.

Keep your hands out of the fries, young man!

But more than this misstep, I remember this:

And these slots are where we slide the hamburgers and fish sandwiches. We sell one every thirty seconds. If thirty minutes should pass without them selling, we throw them away and make new ones.

This—sandbagging—is what I recall most from the field trip. My perception of society somehow changed that day, not because the mean lady wouldn't let me snatch a french fry from the basket, but because it revealed to me the extent to which we devalued the concept of quality and freshness in the foods we ate. Not that it occurred to me then that a regular fast-food diet might be detrimental to my health. Rather, it was the realization that we would deign to eat a hamburger that had been cooked ten or fifteen minutes earlier and that had been sitting for another five or ten. Then again, I was raised to treasure my grandmother's fried chicken, which she cooked Sunday afternoons after church, and which she served up the moment she removed it from the skillet, its aroma tantalizing my nose even as it sizzled between my fingers, still too hot to handle.

As far as I could tell at the time, freshness, wholeness, even temperature didn't appear to factor into our collective decisions about what to eat. What mattered—the *only* thing that seemed to matter, other than cost—was convenience, speed, the ease with which we could collect the food we shoved down our collective gullets. So we could keep working. So we could pay for all those things the media tried to convince us we needed to own. Which kept us working. Which made us, as a nation, fast-food dependent.

Given this, it's no surprise that the concept of organic foods was slow to take root in this country. Mercifully, however, some said they wanted more from their food than empty calories and mere convenience. And there was the mounting evidence that doctors and scientists kept pointing to as they said things like diabetes . . . metabolic syndrome . . . obesity . . . heart disease!

What we were eating was killing us. There must be a better way, we told ourselves, we're still telling ourselves. Enter organic foods. The slow-food movement. Locally grown foods. Chemical-free foods. Clean foods. Nutritious, wholesome foods. Slowly, the concept began to catch on as society better understood the connection between diet and quality of life. We're still catching on.

According to Robin O'Sullivan, author of *American Organic: A Cultural History of Farming, Gardening, Shopping, and Eating*, organic foods began to resonate with many Americans because they emerged as a "key component of countercultural attraction to nutritious cuisine." By the late 1960s and early 1970s, organics had an established following in the United States. This is also the time of a growing ecological awareness among Americans and an increasing resistance to pesticides and other harmful chemicals, attitudes forged partly by the environmental catastrophes of the day, such as the 1969 Santa Barbara oil spill, polluted rivers in our nation's industrial North, the controversy over DDT, and also by America's growing interest in health and wellness—concerns and interests that have more or less prevailed over time.

Though the organic food movement began in the 1940s, for some of us the concept of producing and consuming organics is still new, and many consumers are only now becoming accustomed to regularly seeing these foods in their supermarkets. But interest is growing. Today, organics are available in about 20,000 natural-food markets across the country, according to the USDA, and nearly 75 percent of conventional grocery stores. Most of us consume organic foods, particularly fruits and vegetables, at least occasionally.

With consumer demand expanding, and with a decidedly generic "organic" label beginning to appear more and more frequently on certain foods, thereby complicating our idea of what constituted a food item or growing method termed as such, in 2002 the USDA implemented its National Organic Program (NOP) to regulate organic standards and the accreditation of organic-certifying agents. The NOP defines "organic" as "a labeling term for food or other agricultural products that have been produced using cultural, biological, and mechanical practices that support the cycling of on-farm resources, promote ecological balance, and conserve biodiversity in accordance with the USDA organic regulations," adding that organic operations must maintain or enhance soil and water quality, and conserve wetlands, woodlands, and wildlife.

As to whether the NOP certifies farms, or individuals, it seems it's the latter. When I questioned the USDA about this, I was told that under NOP regulations the certification is issued to the person, but that person may be an individual, partnership, corporation, association, cooperative, or other entity. And as you might expect, certification does not transfer with the sale of a farm or business.

Nuts, of course, are a small part of the nation's overall organic-production pie, and pecans are only a sliver of this. The USDA National Agricultural Statistics Service reports that only twenty-six pecan farms responded to the agency's 2016 Certified Organic Survey. These operations produced 4.7 million pounds of organic pecans from 7,082 acres of trees. Still, as data from the USDA's Economic Research Service confirms, consumer demand for organically produced foods continues to rise, with sales increasing from $13 billion in 2005 to $35 billion in 2014. While economists refer to this trend as "growth," pecan farmers might view it as an opportunity, although relatively few appear to be taking advantage of it. There are several reasons why.

First, and perhaps most important for growers in the eastern half of the pecan belt, is the pecan-scab fungus, for which there is currently no effective organic solution. Then there's the pecan weevil, and while there are organic solutions with which to deal with this pest, they're simply not cost effective. Next is price. The price of conventionally produced pecans is already high—exceedingly high, some say—so there is little incentive for growers to take on the extra work and aggravation in obtaining certification and producing their crop organically when they're already well paid for their conventionally grown pecans. Additionally, becoming a certified organic producer is no simple task. The official handbook for USDA organic regulations contains sections on related terminology and definitions; applicability and exemptions; allowed and prohibited substances, methods, and ingredients; land requirements; soil fertility and crop nutrient management; seeds and planting stock practice; crop rotation; pest, weed, and disease-management practice; and wild-crop harvesting practice. Then there are the annual inspections, which are no trivial matter according to Sally Harper, a certified organic pecan grower and handler and owner of Del Valle Pecans near Las Cruces, New Mexico. "They're not gloss overs," Harper told me in 2017. "They're very involved and take half a day."

Simply put, there are many rules one must follow to become, and remain, a certified organic producer, and as Sally Harper said, most farmers don't like to follow so many rules.

They're nothing new for Harper, though. She's been at this a long time. In the 1980s she and her late husband, Wilmer, bought an orchard of Western Schley pecan trees in the Mesilla Valley of southern New Mexico. They wanted to get out of suburbia and raise organic food for their children. Though her husband worked as an agricultural economist at nearby New Mexico State University, and though they'd had some experience with these trees from living in Oklahoma, growing pecans was no easy task for the Harpers, especially for Sally. Her interest in organics further alienated her from some in her community, like the guy at the tractor parts counter who would barely talk to her, who wouldn't take her seriously.

"It used to be challenging," Sally told me. "It used to irritate me to the ends of the earth. I was a female farmer, and organic to boot. I learned to overlook it. As the years went by it became not much of an issue."

From challenge to challenge, season to season, Sally gradually learned the intricacies of the pecan business, becoming a pioneer in organic production along the way.

Initially, the Harpers sold their organic pecans in the conventional retail market. Sally was eager to explore the organic market, but her husband persuaded her to wait until he could do a feasibility study. While waiting, she shelled and sold thousands of pounds of her pesticide-free pecans. Eventually, she realized that she didn't need a feasibility study. She'd already done it.

Today Del Valle is one of the nation's preeminent growers of organic pecans, producing between 40,000 and 70,000 pounds each year. According to the New Mexico Department of Agriculture, in 2016 there were an estimated 40,000 acres of bearing-age (at least five years old) pecan trees in the state, with seventy-one acres considered organic. Thirty of these organically farmed acres belong to Sally Harper. She grows mostly Western Schley and a few Wichita on Burkett rootstock.

Harper is also a certified handler of organic pecans. She buys from ten to fifteen smaller organic operations in her area and sells them under the Del Valle name. These are hobby farmers mostly, people with a few acres of pecans as a side business, for whom obtaining organic certification may be cost prohibitive or otherwise out of reach. This arrangement allows smaller growers to sell their pecans to Del Valle's established customer base, and it earns them a premium organic price that they couldn't get on their own. As a handler Harper moves 200,000 to 250,000 pounds of organic in-shell pecans each year. She sells 80 percent of her crop directly to retailers, with the other 20 percent split among distributors, bakeries, and restaurants. Her customers, which include a number of smaller health-food stores, as well as the Whole Foods chain, are found throughout the country, from Florida to Washington State, and from Southern California to Maine.

With current retail prices for conventionally produced shelled pecans ranging from $10 to $15 per pound, depending on the retailer and location, it might appear that organics, with their price premium, would be cost prohibitive. This isn't the case. Harper said retail rates for shelled organic pecans range from $17 to $20 per pound, but even at these prices demand outstrips supply. Perhaps for this reason she doesn't feel the need to sell her pecans to China, as so many other growers do.

"My attitude is to supply the US while demand is still here and not mess with overseas paperwork," she said.

Sally believes demand will remain strong as long as prices remain competitive. Given current rates, however, many believe we're well beyond this, although proponents of organic pecans cite the health value and peace of mind that come with eating foods produced naturally and free of pesticides as the real value in buying organics, even over and above that inherent in the pecan itself. To that end, Sally believes the new federal marketing order will ultimately benefit the industry.

"Any information we can get out on the health benefits of pecans is an asset whether they're organic or not," she said. "They are super nutritious. Some don't understand this. They see pecans only in a pie or on top of some little dessert. I understand this. I love pie. But they are much more than a dessert food. They are a superfood."

Today Sally runs Del Valle Pecans with the assistance of her daughter Laura and son Todd. She has one full-time employee in the orchard, two more in the office, and another for tractor maintenance, weeding, pruning, and those tasks Sally said she's no longer inclined to do. She sold her harvesting equipment to her son, who now runs a custom harvesting business with a crew of about ten. The drivers, one of whom is Todd himself, remain with the staff each year, while the ground crew, who run the leaf blowers, rakes, and other equipment, come and go from season to season. Sally said staffing the ground crew is often challenging. The best way is word of mouth.

"Once one guy is on, he has a buddy or a family member that needs a job," she said. "This is the best way to find good help. There are some labor brokers. They work okay. I used a labor service once, but that didn't work out. They wanted to work only half a day, and then leave to go get their check. Sometimes we advertise on Craigslist. We've found a few good workers here. We had some young high school and college kids once. They were super. When they graduated, they got jobs. Now I scramble for a good ground crew each year."

Sally's perseverance through more than thirty years in a career that's physically and emotionally demanding, weather dependent, and highly unpredictable is inspiring. It's also a testament to her strength and tenacity. I asked her if she thought she was convincing some of her peers to grow pecans organically.

"Maybe locally, yes," she said, "because they've seen that my orchard didn't die or that my production didn't tank. I think they look at it different or in a more softened view, that maybe we don't need all the chemicals we put on the trees and push into our groundwater."

Sally's success over the years has proven it. So has her staying power.

"You just persist and keep going back and talking to them," she said of those early detractors who ultimately failed to discourage her, failed to distract her. "They find out you're a human being, and it doesn't matter anymore. They come around, but it takes some time," she said. "Like twenty years."

Unlike the US almond and walnut industries, which are centered in California, the pecan industry stretches across the southern United States, from the hair-frizzing humidity of the Carolinas, across the hot and windy southern plains, through the desert Southwest and all the way to California's world-feeding Central Valley. When you consider the range of topographies and climates that the pecan belt encompasses, you begin to understand that farmers in North Carolina face very different challenges from those in Kansas, those in New Mexico, and those in California. Nowhere is this more apparent than with the issue of water. A geographer might look at a map of the United States and say that the line of demarcation is the 100th meridian, that imaginary barrier separating most of Oklahoma (excluding the panhandle) from the Texas panhandle and often said to separate the American West from the rest of the nation. I think Interstate 35 is a better divider. This strip of pavement separates two very different regions—the terminus of the eastern deciduous forest and the beginning of the great western plains. It also bisects the ecotone encompassing this border region, as along I-35 you'll find flora and fauna from either of these disparate habitats intermingling as they have for millennia. Head off in either direction, east or west, however, and the landscape and climate soon change considerably.

Interstate 35 also intersects the Cross Timbers, that unique forest of rugged post oak and blackjack oak trees extending from southeastern Kansas through central and eastern Oklahoma and deep into Texas. Precipitation drops quickly as you move west within the Cross Timbers. Annual rainfall averages forty inches in the east, while the western Cross Timbers region sees about twenty-five inches. And we're not even to the 100th meridian yet. Although this is twice the average annual rainfall for the state of Arizona, for example, it by no means suggests adequate water for pecan growing as rain events here can be few and far between, with summers that are typically scorching. Indeed, this paltry two feet of annual rainfall hints at the irrigation challenges facing pecan farmers here in the near Southwest, and the problem compounds the farther west we go. Given this, it's easy to understand Mary Austin's thoughts in *The Land of Little Rain* (1903), in which she writes, "It is the proper destiny of every considerable stream in the West to become an irrigating ditch."

Water, of course, is the limiting element for agriculture in the Southwest. Most of it comes from two primary sources. In the far Southwest it is the Colorado River. In New Mexico it's the Rio Grande. Elephant Butte Reservoir, an impoundment of the Rio Grande near the community of Truth or Consequences, New Mexico, stores water used for agricultural irrigation farther downstream. As long as there is sufficient snowpack in the mountains of northern New Mexico and southern Colorado, the Rio Grande is a welcome source of irrigation. But during prolonged droughts farmers turn to groundwater pumping, which can lead to aquifer depletion.

In the arid Southwest, water is diverted from the Colorado and Rio Grande rivers to agricultural fields through irrigation channels and floodgates, through which it infiltrates the orchards and fields, and gradually seeps into the soil, a process on which Mary Austin reflected, more than one hundred years ago, when she noted, "It is difficult to come into intimate relations with appropriated waters; like very busy people they have no time to reveal themselves." Inevitably, like certain people who flow in and out of our lives, some of this water evaporates, and for this reason many farmers now rely on drip systems, precision sprinklers, and pipe irrigation to make the most of what swirls into their arid worlds—what's here today and by tomorrow perhaps gone away. Also, commercial pecan growers today laser-level their orchard floors until they're as flat as billiard tables to prevent runoff. All these measures help southwestern farmers make the most efficient use of what is in the best of times a limited resource.

As in Arizona, agriculture accounts for most of New Mexico's water use. In 2010 this amounted to over three million acre-feet (78 percent) of total withdrawals, according to a report by the Water Use and Conservation Bureau of the New Mexico Office of the State Engineer. Growing pecans is an inherently water-intensive pursuit, and western orchards don't receive the abundant rainfall that pecan trees in the Southeast do. In light of this, one wonders about the future of pecan farming in this hot, dry region. And yet, some of the ideas for adapting to water shortages are encouraging.

In a 2011 report from the Stockholm Environmental Institute, economists Frank Ackerman and Elizabeth Stanton addressed the disparity between water supply in the Southwest and the projected demand for this resource. One solution they proposed involves prioritizing specific agricultural crops according to their ability to convert water to food and, ultimately, dollars. The economists suggested that reducing our dependence on crops that return comparatively little value on our water investment could be one way to reduce demand on the resource. They added that it would have little impact on US or world agricultural markets while helping balance water supply.

This sounds reasonable enough, but which crops are the most important? More specifically, which deliver the greatest value from the water we invest in them?

The economists ranked Southwest agricultural crops according to their dollar value per acre-foot of water used to grow them, while noting that one acre-foot of water is considered enough to meet the annual needs of two four-member families.

According to the report, nursery and greenhouse products fared best, earning $28,000 per acre-foot of water. Fruits, vegetables, and nuts were far behind, but they still fared well relative to some of the other crops, producing sales above $1,000 per acre-foot. Cotton, wheat, corn, and other grains scored low, however, reflecting values under $500 per acre-foot. Hay was even lower, $121 on average, although the economists noted that this is grown primarily to feed livestock.

Compounding all of this, of course, is climate change, which scientists tell us will result in less precipitation over time and ultimately less water for any use. Droughts, they say, will become more intense and last longer. Higher air temperatures will translate into greater water loss through evaporation. These warmer temperatures will also lead to mountain runoff earlier in the year and will ultimately reduce river flows later in the year during the growing season, when this water is most needed. This is true for the entire Southwest, particularly Arizona and Southern California, which are home to some of the nation's largest and fastest-growing cities, such as Los Angeles and Phoenix. Currently, 40 million people in this arid corner of the country depend on water from the Colorado River, which today runs dry long before its traditional confluence with the Gulf of California in northwest Mexico. In 1922 conservationist Aldo Leopold and his brother canoed what was then a vast Colorado River delta teeming with fish and wildlife, later describing his adventure in an essay entitled "The Green Lagoons." Today, the formerly 3,000-square-mile delta covers less than

250 square miles. Save for heavy rains, the only water flowing through it is runoff from alfalfa, lettuce and melon fields, and pecan orchards.

This morning I received a message on my phone. It was from Kyle. He told me the refuge had gone a week or two without rain and as a result the floodwaters had finally receded, allowing access to the champion pecan tree. If I wanted to come down and see it, he'd be happy to drive me out to the tree.

Wonderful! I thought.

The only problem is, I'm out of town, out of state, on the East Coast.

I considered ending my trip early so I could get back to Oklahoma and see the tree before the next rainfall. Was I being unreasonable? Probably. After all, the big pecan had been there for a long time and hopefully would remain there for many years to come. I didn't have to see the tree right away, but I wanted to. I was tired of waiting, and by this point I had seen enough cultivated trees to realize they held no charm or special allure for me. Wild trees, on the other hand, were different, especially ancient ones. Of these old trees Aldo Leopold once wrote that he who owns one also owns "a historical library, and a reserved seat in the theatre of evolution." This is certainly how I felt about the champion pecan, in part because it was so old, and also because it was a product of Mother Nature.

I'm not the only person fascinated by wild pecans. In his book, *The Last Wild Places of Kansas*, George Frazier writes of being "intrigued" by the groves of native pecan trees along the Marais des Cygnes River in eastern Kansas:

> I never knew pecans were native to Kansas, and while pawpaws and persimmons were substantial fruits, nobody ate them (or even knew what they were) in the suburbs where I grew up. Even though pecans were commonly available, the thought of wild pecan groves seemed

exotic, like sunken steamboats buried in farm fields along the Missouri River. More incredibly, I learned that some existing groves might predate settlement; in other words, trees growing today along the Marais des Cygnes might have provided shade for the Osage and French fur trappers plying the River of the Swans in sweet gum pirogues. The thought was electrifying.

I remember feeling similarly intrigued about the Oklahoma champion pecan tree the first time I viewed it. Like Frazier, part of my fascination stemmed from the big pecan's history, which certainly predated Oklahoma statehood, and the thought that it might have sprouted from the ground around the time the American Civil War ended, or maybe even before the war. Also, it had grown through the succeeding decades with no human interference and despite the development that has proven detrimental to other wild trees and groves throughout the pecan's native landscape. This old tree was certainly graceful, resilient, and magical even. But perhaps more than anything else it was a survivor.

Frazier seems beset with a similar sense of wonder, even mild incredulity, that wild pecan trees might yet survive, overlooked or forgotten, in his home state of Kansas. He recognizes that entering a grove of ancient pecan trees would be like "walking back into a lost era," and he's energized by the thought that wild stands of these survivors are out there waiting to be rediscovered. Alas, however, Frazier writes that he was unable to locate any such stands of old pecans along the Marais des Cygnes.

Sometime later, his zeal for discovering ancient pecans intact, Frazier travels with a small group to the "Holy Grail of Kansas forests," the Fort Leavenworth Woods. US military bases are often bastions of biodiversity for the simple fact that vast tracts of these facilities have been under federal control for many decades and have avoided development. Like other communities, military bases have their high-use areas and networks of roads and thoroughfares, but many of them also have expansive tracts that see little or no human disturbance. Preserved over many years, the biotic communities of these areas remain diverse and largely intact. I recall the remote "back side" of Camp Lejeune, North Carolina, where I spent a lot of time during my service in the US Marine Corps. There must have been thousands of acres of coastal forest and savanna in this immense section of the base, and other than an occasional trail from which an Abrams tank would sometimes appear, moving at a high rate of speed, this area saw extremely limited human activity. As a result, it was refreshingly peaceful and largely undisturbed.

Another base where I spent time and received most of my military training, Marine Corps Base Camp Pendleton, in Southern California, which encompasses more than 125,000 acres, is home to the federally endangered Pacific pocket mouse. This tiny mouse was thought to be extinct until it was rediscovered in 1993 at the nearby Dana Point Headlands and, shortly thereafter, at Camp Pendleton. Along with the sixty-acre Dana Point Headlands Conservation Area, Camp Pendleton, which includes the largest tracts of undeveloped coastline in Southern California, has proven a vital refuge for this species.

Frazier writes that the bottomland forests surrounding Fort Leavenworth are similarly remote and undeveloped. When his party came upon a woodland marsh with a thick understory, he was once again forced to abandon his search for the ancient pecan groves. He didn't forget about them though. Returning to the base during hunting season, he continued his search, this time while wearing blaze-orange safety gear. He followed a deer path deep into the forest until at last he came upon the majestic old pecans, a "virgin forest spiraling upward in stages" that "functioned as a self-contained system nourishing plants and animals that kept the ancient processes going, that *were* the ancient processes, filling their own larder, self-creating but for sunlight and time."

Experiencing groves of old-growth pecan trees is a special experience, one that puts today's commercial orchards into the proper perspective, one that reminds you that these wild trees have been here much longer than we have and that they're survivors, worthy of the time it takes to find and experience them—and to protect these increasingly rare ecosystems. Too, I think it's symbolic that when we find these ancient trees, very often we find a grove of them, as if these holdouts from modernity and development find strength and resolve in like-minded company, as if they're showing us what can happen when kindred spirits stick together.

Along with these undisturbed Kansas trees, one can find many acres of wild pecans growing just across the state line, in southwestern Missouri. Here, along the Osage, Little Osage, Marmaton, and Marais des Cygnes Rivers and their tributaries, are thousands of acres of ideal pecan-growing habitat. What surprised me, however, was that this area is something of a center for organic pecan production. Drew Kimmell, one farmer I spoke to, grows eighty acres of pecans along the Big Dry Wood Creek near Nevada, Missouri, on land his father purchased in the 1970s. Kimmell said most of his trees are wild but added that his father grafted a few of them forty years ago, when farmers in southwest Missouri were just beginning to experiment with this process. One mistake many of them made was using pecan varieties adapted to a southern climate. Kimmell said southwest Missouri had a "mini Ice Age" in the late 1970s, killing these southern trees. The experience helped growers in his area understand that they needed northern tree varieties. The wild trees? They've stood their ground all these years, and they're still here. According to the US Department of Agriculture, Vernon County, Missouri, averaged nearly fifty inches of annual precipitation during the years 1981–2010, which means unlike the Southwest, water isn't normally an issue here. It's reliable enough that Kimmell says he doesn't provide his trees with any supplemental irrigation, although in particularly wet years it can exacerbate the issue of pecan scab. When I asked Kimmell if scab was his greatest challenge as a grower of organic pecans, he said no. This distinction goes to the pecan's alternate-bearing tendency. "I've been in the pecan business off and on for thirty to forty years," Kimmell said. "In that time you realize that pecans are alternate-bearing, and you deal with it. Alternate-bearing is a factor you take into account."

Kimmell said he manages his trees in a style that's low input and nonintensive. He prunes limbs and sprouts, removes vines, and cuts the grass in his grove. But he doesn't practice topping or hedging, which he says necessitates supplemental fertilization and irrigation. Instead, he prefers to grow his pecans as naturally as possible. "I know what I'm selling my customer," he said. "I know I'm not spraying them with detrimental chemicals."

I asked Kimmell what made him want to take on the additional paperwork and endure the inspections that come with organic certification. He told me it was the premium that organic pecans command in the market. "We input almost nothing but we get a better price," he said.

Who can argue with this?

Although only seven Missouri farms responded to the USDA's 2016 certified organic survey—more than any other state—Kimmell said there were twenty-five to thirty other organic growers in Vernon County. Why so many? I wondered. Why are so many farmers here in Vernon County willing to take on the additional headache of obtaining and maintaining organic certification? Was it simply for the additional income? Or was there some other reason?

I spoke with Joe Wilson, general manager of Missouri Northern Organic Pecans, who told me that many farmers in southwest Missouri were already growing pecans organically—due to a lack of tree management—when his organization began approaching them in 2003 about going organic. The incentive for the growers was a higher organic price, and by working together as a collective, they're able to

Roadside pecan stands such as this one are a common sight across the US pecan belt in autumn and early winter. They allow producers to sell their product directly to consumers, who value the opportunity to purchase the freshest pecans.

provide a steadier supply of product than a farmer working alone. That first year, seventeen growers signed up to join the collective. Today, Missouri Northern Organic Pecans has fifty members working a total of 3,800 acres of organic pecans in Vernon and southern Bates counties. The largest individual operation is 300 acres; there are many members with twenty- to forty-acre groves. Ninety percent of the organization's organic pecans are produced from native trees.

Wilson said that because of the area's northern growing range, pests and diseases aren't as problematic as they are for southern growers. This includes pecan scab, which he said isn't normally an issue for his farmers. He finds the best way to prevent it is to allow ample air flow between trees, which necessitates thinning and pruning on occasion. Wilson told me he had just purchased eighty acres with many pecan trees, although they were located in thickly wooded areas. He said he was planning to remove the other trees so that he could open up the grove for better pecan production.

Residents of the Show-Me State who are seeking to plant a few pecan trees on their property have a tremendous resource in the George O. White State Forest Nursery, located near the small town of Licking, in the Ozarks. Owned by the Missouri Department of Conservation, the nursery grows over sixty species of trees and shrubs, which are offered to residents as seedlings for reforestation, windbreaks, erosion control, wildlife cover and food, and for planting as shade trees. Each year, the nursery processes 10,000 orders and ships roughly four million seedlings to residents across the state. One of these tree species is the pecan, which is grown primarily from seeds from native Missouri trees. I phoned with several questions and was told that for the 2017 season the nursery had purchased 3,000 pounds of these seeds, which produced an estimated 75,000 pecan seedlings. The nursery grows these seedlings for one year. When they reach the twelve- to twenty-four-inch range, the young trees are shipped.

In its description of the pecan, the Missouri Department of Conservation lists some of the tree's characteristics—flowers April–May; fruits September–October in clusters of three to ten nuts; grows to heights of 130 feet—along with information on the pecan's range, etymology, history, and a few recipes, including pecan-crusted crappie. The department also provides information on some places to see pecan trees in Missouri: 1) Bruns (Dr. Bernard) Access: a small conservation area southeast of Jefferson City in central Missouri; 2) the Douglas Branch Conservation Area: a 511-acre bottomland woodland and wet prairie in southwestern Missouri that Audubon Missouri has designated as an "important bird area"; 3) the Edmonson Access on Cole Camp Creek: a tributary of Lake of the Ozarks, in central Missouri; 4) General Watkins Conservation Area: 1,000 acres of mostly forest habitat in Scott County, in the southeastern corner of the state, just north of the Missouri Bootheel; and 5) Hazel Hill Lake: 500 acres of fields, grasslands, and forest in the central part of the state.

Then I learned the nursery shipped its seedlings even to those outside Missouri. So I decided to order a few and look for a place to plant them the following spring, reasoning that they might enhance the genetic diversity (and perhaps also the cold tolerance) of one of my area's native groves. At the very least I would plant a few new seedlings that would hopefully outlive me and, with any luck, constitute a future food source for local wildlife.

When I called to check on the availability of pecan seedlings, a recorded message informed me that the nursery had already received 5,300 orders. Then it named several species that were out of stock—black gum, black haw, elderberry, flowering dogwood, hazelnut, Kentucky coffee tree, pawpaw, persimmon, sassafras, serviceberry, and several others. Fortunately, I did not hear "pecan" listed, so I placed my order for ten seedlings to be delivered in the spring of the new year.

—8—

Assets and Liabilities

In an April 10, 2017, blog entry on the website northernpecans.com, Kansas pecan scientist Bill Reid writes about how soil type affects pecan bud break. The greater the clay content of a soil, he writes, the slower that soil warms in the spring.

Reid adds that cold soil inhibits the growth of new roots, and he points out that slower root activity delays the onset of bud break.

An accompanying photo shows two Kanza twig samples taken on the same day, from trees growing only 500 yards apart. The one with minimal bud break was taken from a tree growing in what Reid calls Osage silty clay. The twig with greater bud break was taken from a tree growing in something called Cherokee silt loam.

The Osage soil is a true river-bottom gumbo soil, Reid writes, while the Cherokee soil is a lighter-textured second-bottom soil. He notes that both soils originated as river-deposited sediments, but that the Osage has greater clay content.

Recently I attended a forest-ecology workshop at Oklahoma State University, where I was given a soil-texture-triangle chart. Besides being very interesting, this chart is useful for determining an orchard's soil type. If I understand it correctly, because soil is composed of three major elements—clay, silt, and sand—we can determine the texture of a specific soil by measuring the relative composition of these elements. According to the chart, a soil containing 70 percent sand, for example, and 10 percent clay, is classified as sandy loam. As we lose more of the sand, and as silt replaces clay, we get a silty loam. A soil with 50 percent sand composition and the remainder balanced more or less evenly between clay and silt is a medium loam.

This is an example of the type of fun you can have with a soil-texture-triangle chart. It's perfect for rainy days, sleepless nights, or those long, trans-pecan-belt road trips.

Equipped with such technology, an aspiring pecan producer may find his confidence growing and perhaps wish to build on this knowledge with a more comprehensive soil test, which can identify potential mineral deficiencies. This information can inform how one manages his pecan holdings, especially with regard to fertilizing. After all, unless we know exactly what's in the soil, we're playing a guessing game when we apply fertilizer.

Soil tests like this are available from university-based extension services throughout the pecan belt. The process is so simple that even a writer, someone who's never grown a single pecan tree, could gather up a suitable sample and deliver it for testing with the assurance that the forthcoming analysis will reflect that soil's composition, and any mineral deficiencies, with a tremendous level of precision. And this offers a certain peace of mind.

Instructions for obtaining such a sample might look something like this:

1. Using a small spade or shovel, collect a sample of soil, taking care to dig to a depth of approximately six inches.
2. Deposit this sample into a clean bucket.

3. Repeat this process twelve to fifteen times, taking samples from different locations within the specified area, and depositing each sample into the same clean bucket.
4. Mix these collected soil deposits together.
5. Fill two cups with this soil mixture and pour them into a clean container.
6. Bring this representative sample to your county extension office or other soil authority, along with a check for whatever nominal fee is required.
7. Return home. Enjoy a glass of lemonade. Pop a few pecans. Await your soil analysis, which should arrive by mail in only a few short weeks, along with recommendations for fertilizer and any soil amendments.

In addition to the soil analysis, which is perhaps one of the simplest and most common ways that science is helping to produce stronger pecan crops, today growers are turning to other, more sophisticated forms of technology to better manage their holdings. This includes, among others, remote imaging and data acquisition. One company specializing in this is Florida-based AGERpoint™, which describes itself as an agriculture farming solution using cutting edge technology. The company's CEO and founder, Tom McPeek, is a former architect who specialized in the use of LiDAR (Light Detection and Ranging, a remote sensing technology utilizing laser light to collect three-dimensional point clouds of the earth's surface) to document buildings for renovation and historic preservation. In 2012 McPeek leveraged his background in sensors and computer modeling to develop a phenotyping solution for a citrus grower who was seeking a better way to manage his orchard.

"He asked if we could use lasers to document his entire citrus field," McPeek told me during a 2017 interview. "He wanted to be able to predict his yield. So we developed a mobile system we could mount to a vehicle and drive up and down the rows to create a point cloud of each tree, which is made up of hundreds of thousands of points. This technology can extract the entire morphology of a tree—the size of the trunk and canopy, its location, and the size and number of fruit on the tree."

This information is combined with photographic data from spectral imaging—which can identify specific cultivars as well as the presence of any existing disease or fungus, for example—and entered into an online portal that provides growers with information they need to better manage their crops.

The technology McPeek developed now forms the basis for his company's product line, which includes a mobile-friendly LiDAR sensor developed using military-grade technology, a comprehensive crop information-management system with mapping interface, and technology that provides both location and phenotype data for each specific tree within an orchard.

Though initially developed for the citrus industry, McPeek said his company is now working with pecan growers who want to inventory their trees.

"Understanding your holdings can help determine what the yield might be," McPeek told me. "Our technology helps growers validate the farming techniques they're using. Like hedging and topping, which are becoming very popular. Growers want to know whether these technologies make sense, and whether they should be deployed the way they are with other crops. We're finding that topping makes a lot of sense. There are limitations on what sprayers can do, for example. Controlling black fungus is a real issue, and topping helps do this. Having all this data helps growers understand the effectiveness of farming technologies and techniques. It also helps in understanding the location of different tree varieties within a field. For growers in

Georgia, for example, it's not uncommon to have six or eight varieties in one field. Having this information helps them plan their strategy for managing different areas of their orchard."

When I asked McPeek if his data-gathering technology was deployed through drones, he said it was but added that drones are only one tool in the toolbox.

"We use the same sensors on the ground as we do in the air," he said. "We look at which is the most appropriate tool. In some cases, this means using more than one type of technology."

McPeek said the LiDAR system's ability to gather data and form a comprehensive point cloud is based on two things: the speed of travel through which it's deployed and the sensor's distance from the object it is surveying. The slower the sensing unit travels and the closer it is deployed to the surveyed object, the higher the point density (and the more data acquired).

"For example, to count the number of grapes on a vine cluster: I can do this if I go low and slow," McPeek told me. "An aerial drone can fly over the vineyard, but it won't be able to count the number of grapes on the vines because it's going too fast."

Compared with soil testing, this is more like rocket science. But both types of technologies are being used to improve today's pecan production.

Many years ago, to supplement the ashtray change I earned in my first few years as a freelance writer, I took a side job. As writing required me to be indoors, at a desk, in front of one of those silly gadgets that consume so much of our time and attention and to which society seems powerless to overcome its addiction, I wanted to do something completely different with my part-time gig. I craved physical labor. And most of all, I wanted to be outdoors.

One day I was driving down the street when I passed a feed store with a sign out front: "Help Wanted." I walked inside, and five minutes later I had a job. A side job. A steady paycheck.

One of the basic functions, and refreshing benefits, of this gig was the opportunity to sling feed, fifty pounds at a time. In hardly any time at all, I developed muscular shoulders. I could balance two fifty-pound bags of feed on either shoulder, so that I frequently carried my own weight around. It was great exercise, and after many hours sitting inside my home office, in front of that silly electronic gizmo that, regrettably, has absolutely hypnotized humanity, slinging feed was liberating, even empowering. Sometimes it was also dangerous.

Once I was driving the company truck to deliver five hundred pounds of rolled oats to a customer with horses. To get to the horse ranch I had to drive through a part of town whose best days, if there had ever been any good ones at all, had deteriorated along with the district's infrastructure. It was high noon on a busy weekday, and as I approached this district's most heavily traveled intersection the brakes on the old feed-store jalopy suddenly sank to the floor. I pumped the pedal. Nothing.

Cross-traffic streamed through the street in front of me like a forbidding river current. What to do? There was no time to think. I was already at the busy intersection.

I did the only thing I could do. I spun the steering wheel as sharply, quickly, and as decisively as I could. I think I put the pickup truck on two wheels as I carved that street corner. Somehow, mercifully, I managed to miss the oncoming traffic. Unfortunately, however, the load of oats I was delivering slid off the pickup truck's flatbed and into the street.

I coasted down the hill, pumping the brake pedal, but to no avail. I was headed for a crash landing. I just needed a clear open space where I could put this old bucket of bolts down without endangering anyone else. And I spotted it. Just ahead there was a defunct discount store. I rolled into the vacant parking lot and bumped into a curb, where at last I was able to bring the out-of-control vehicle to a halt. Looking back at the intersection, I noticed traffic had stopped. Sitting in the middle, beneath the traffic light, was a car. It was one of those old sedans that might easily be mistaken for a river barge. Its doors were open. Four men were grabbing the bags of oats and throwing them inside. Poof! Thud! One after another. The men were running with the loot. They were moving with urgency. I couldn't see their faces. But I knew what they were thinking. *Gold! We found something! It's our lucky day!*

Then they jumped inside and the car, now sagging like a pair of baggy pants, lumbered through the intersection and disappeared in a billowing cloud of exhaust like a smoke screen designed to help the men escape.

At this point, considering I'd managed to avoid crashing, I was happy just to be alive. I didn't care about the oats. Besides, the laugh was on them. Unless those four fellows owned horses, their booty was worthless. However, had it been late autumn and had the cargo been the load of pecans I might have hauled, these pavement pirates would have had something to celebrate. That's because, unlike oats, pecans are valuable. And it seems everyone knows it.

With current wholesale prices for pecans exceeding three dollars a pound for many varieties, and with retail prices pushing fifteen dollars a pound in some areas, these nuts are like money falling from trees. And while this is a boon for growers, it's also an enticement for thieves. One Georgia farmer reported thousands of dollars in losses to thieves over the course of a single season, while another recalled spending Thanksgiving Day tracking down a looter in his orchard. Evidently, the looter had brought a bathtub with him, but he wasn't interested in cleaning up his act.

Today's pecan growers face many threats, not least of which are pecan thieves.

"When I caught up with him, he said he was gathering nuts for a pie," the farmer explained to a reporter. "I told him he was a long way from the pumpkin grove."

Unfortunately, these cases aren't unique. Authorities across the nation are investigating more pecan thefts, including many felony-grade thefts. A couple of thieves with buckets or bags—or a bathtub—can seriously impact a grower's bottom line. This is particularly problematic for small growers, who operate with extremely narrow margins. Not surprisingly, law-enforcement agencies treat these crimes seriously. So do farmers. Many are now monitoring their orchards with remote cameras, drones, dogs, and their own security staff.

It seemed every pecan farmer I spoke to had his own version of a Great Pecan Heist. One of the most interesting came from a Georgia grower who told me about his security guard catching a man ramming one of the company's pecan trees with a pickup truck. "He was

This Texas golf course is surrounded by large pecan trees.

trying to knock down the pecans so he could steal them," he told me. Evidently, the thief didn't mind sacrificing his vehicle's front bumper and grill in order to do so.

But pecan thefts aren't limited to orchards. I interviewed a bakery owner in St. Louis who told me of losing this key ingredient to thieves.

"We had five locations then, so we were a large enough operation that we ordered our pecans in bulk," he told me. "We bought them from the Natchez Pecan Shelling Company in Mississippi. They were quality pecans. We didn't scrimp on ingredients or cost. We were paying a hundred and fifty dollars for a thirty-pound case. During the holidays, when we were really busy, we might have ten or twenty cases sitting around the bakery. That's a lot of money for a small organization."

And an enticement for unscrupulous (or hungry) thieves.

"We couldn't pinpoint who was taking them," he said, "but we knew they were disappearing."

I asked this man, whose name is Michael, if the thieves swiped any other types of ingredients. Walnuts, say? Chocolate chips? Crisco shortening?

It turns out: no, no, and no. These thieves were discerning. They wanted only the pecans.

"Finally, we had to number the boxes so we could keep track of how many were being used," Michael explained. "We had the bakers place each empty box beside the head baker so he could keep track of how many were being used day to day."

"Did this work?" I asked.

"Once we began numbering the boxes, the thefts stopped," he said.

Unfortunately, the rising costs of running a small business haven't. Michael has since closed his bakeries.

Everyone knows that squirrels love pecans. Recently, I was reminded just how much they relish these nuts. I keep a bird feeder in my backyard, which attracts a variety of species throughout the year. The black-oil sunflower seeds I set out in winter help the birds survive the cold, and watching them helps me get through these gloomy, gray months. In spring and summer the supplemental fruit-and-seed blend provides extra sustenance for nesting birds, who add so much color and life to my backyard.

Squirrels used to be a problem, as they love this fruit-and-seed mixture. Not long ago, however, while visiting Brett Mason's store in Norman, Oklahoma, I bought a bag of his "squirrel food." Each day I toss a handful of these second-class pecans on the ground around my bird feeder. Since I've been doing this, the squirrels have completely ignored the birdseed. Not only this, but I've noticed that the blue jays, and even the brown thrashers, enjoy these nuts. The jays drop to the ground, take a nut in their beak, and fly away to eat it, while the thrashers give the kernels a good thrashing before devouring them.

More problematic than squirrels, however, are crows. In Oklahoma we have a lot of them. Crows are perhaps the most intelligent of all birds, and they live in sophisticated social structures that almost always include lookout birds who provide a measure of security and peace of mind for the flock. They seem to know as well as growers, and sometimes even better, when pecan crops are maturing. This large, muscular bird is often said to have a preference for thin-shelled pecans, which makes sense. But crows are so intelligent that they've been observed using tools to help them procure their dinner. For example, researchers have recorded crows using sticks to capture ants. The birds take up sticks in their beaks and then lower them into ant colonies. When the sticks are crawling with ants, the crows remove them and dinner is served.

Not long ago, while staying in a California hotel whose well-manicured grounds overlooking the Pacific Ocean provided a relaxing respite from the busy traffic on the nearby Coast Highway, and evidently a smorgasbord for local wildlife, I had the opportunity to witness over the course of a single weekend the intelligence and ingenuity of the American crow. Throughout the day on Friday, I had noticed a team of gardeners hard at work, planting some type of small succulent in a tiered flower bed along the hotel's southern perimeter. The gardeners had the following weekend off work, however, and while they were away the crows came out for breakfast, lunch, and dinner. Over the next two days I watched these big birds traipsing through the flower bed and extracting the same succulents the gardeners had spent the previous Friday planting. Taking the main stem into their beaks, the crows would give a tug or two and out came the plant, revealing a shallow pocket evidently crawling in grubworms or some other insect delicacy. Only once did I observe a crow give up on a plant that refused to be extracted after a series of short tugs. Save for this single succulent, the crows spent the weekend unearthing every other plant the gardeners had set out, and they probably fattened up in the process.

Crows have been observed slamming nuts against rocks and other hard surfaces in order to crack them. Given this, even a thick shell doesn't present much of an obstacle for a bird with this level of intelligence, size, strength, and determination.

Recently, however, I learned there is a variety of pecan they often avoid, and that's the Caddo.

Caddo pecans have a sharp point on either end of the shell. Charles Rohla says that when crows get this variety in their beaks, it pokes them. "So they stay clear," he says.

Rohla tells of an Oklahoma pecan farmer who plants several varieties, most of which are highly attractive to these birds.

"The crows will pick his Pawnees apart," he says. "Once they get all the Pawnees, they'll move into his Kanza. But Kanza isn't their first choice. But they're hardly ever in his Caddo crop."

Then there are wild hogs, a growing nuisance across much of the pecan belt. They're so problematic that annual pecan-growing conferences regularly feature workshops on managing feral hogs. These animals damage pecan and other agricultural crops, and they're a threat to young livestock. One study estimated these losses in Texas alone at more than $52 million each year. Mississippi State University even has a microsite dedicated to feral hogs, with information on their history, behavior, and biology, and their management through hunting and trapping.

Traps for feral hogs range from wooden crate-style boxes featuring sliding doors to expansive, corral-style pens that allow the capture and retention of multiple animals. One model called the BoarBuster™, developed at the Noble Research Institute in Oklahoma, features a large, circular corral enclosure that's suspended several feet above the ground. The BoarBuster™ is designed to send text or e-mail messages upon motion activation, and it can be monitored and triggered through one's cell phone anywhere with Internet service. It also streams live video through a designated web server. This technology eliminates nontargeted animals from being captured while helping mitigate the considerable economic and ecological damage that feral hogs cause.

Prior to one recent pecan workshop I attended, talk among the audience members centered on hunting rifles and heavy-gauge wire traps. Both, it turned out, were being discussed in the context of controlling the local feral-hog population, which was described as out of control. One grower told of trapping a couple of the animals in his orchard one recent night, but he had decided to wait until morning, and daylight, to dispatch them. (It seems he was able to monitor his trap through a remotely mounted game camera.) When he showed up the following morning, rifle in hand, the hogs had escaped.

Recently, after watching a German shepherd pick up native pecans off the ground, crack them open with her teeth, and eat them, I began wondering whether coyotes do the same when presented with the opportunity. They're omnivorous, after all, and if the food is available it seems reasonable that they would eat it. Bill Reid's *Northern Pecans* blog post of November 8, 2017, entitled "Who's Eating My Pecans?," lists the coyote as one of several species known to consume this nut. But for an animal who has resisted society's best efforts to eradicate it—and has even expanded its range in the process—why should this be a surprise?

Even more problematic than mammals are insects because they consume and destroy not only the nut but also pecan leaves and twigs, thereby undermining the pecans themselves. Chief among them is the pecan nut casebearer (PNC). According to Texas A&M AgriLife Extension specialist Bill Ree, it's the number-one insect pest for pecans. And this is saying something, for among insects Ree says some 20 different varieties feed on pecan nuts, 103 eat the tree's foliage, and 67 insect species devour pecan tree twigs, branches, and roots.

"The pecan nut casebearer is basically the reason I have a job," Ree told an assembly at a recent pecan pest-management seminar.

Adult PNC moths are gray, about a third of an inch in length, with dark scales on their forewings. Mating and egg deposition occur at night, after tree pollination. During their weeklong lifespan, females can produce dozens of eggs, which are laid on the pecan nuts.

The PNC produces three generations each year. It's the first that is likely to be the most problematic if not controlled, especially during light crop years when trees carry fewer pecans. This is because first-generation larvae feed on the pecan nuts themselves. Second- and third-generation casebearers, appearing later in the summer, feed mostly on pecan shucks and cause much less damage.

Ree says the key to managing the pecan nut casebearer is being proactive. For this reason he emphasizes the importance of monitoring for the insect, a job he says is best performed with a 10x magnifying lens. He identifies the most opportune time to apply the pesticide by placing pheromone-scented traps in an orchard, ideally before even the first PNC is spotted.

The time from the first PNC sighting to the egg-laying stage is only seven days. And from here the insect's entry into nut clusters is only fourteen days. Having this information and knowing the residual period for the specific pesticide used helps growers determine the most effective time to spray, which Ree says must be done only once. Miss the window by a few weeks and this prolific insect can make short work of a pecan crop. Time it right and you can then turn your attention to protecting your pecans from feral hogs, blue jays, crows, and other pests.

—9—

The American Pecan

March. Nearly April, in fact. Spring has already sprung here in the Sonoran Desert. Or, warm as it is, maybe it has been here all along. If winter exists at all here in this beautifully desolate and prickly landscape south of Tucson, near the United States–Mexico border, there's no sign of it today. The sun blazes down from the vast blue sky with the intensity of a welding torch as it torches the cactus and scrub brush–cluttered expanses paralleling the Old Nogales Highway on which I'm traveling to a gathering of the nation's pecan shellers in the tiny village of Tubac, an oasis of sorts, where I'm scheduled to attend Dan Zedan's presentation on pecan exports and global production. Gravel and grit pepper the undercarriage of the fifteen-passenger Ford van, a vintage 80s model whose air conditioner groans as it struggles to keep the cavernous cabin cool, and whose bulging center console is so protuberant and obtrusive that I have to sit cockeyed in the passenger seat to have any legroom. Mountains loom in the distance to the east, while in the west a giant copper mine hides just over the rise.

After driving for miles through a mostly open desert landscape, a landscape accented with clumps of cactus and tumbleweed-looking jumbles of kindling-dry brush and the occasional mesquite tree, but with its natural sightlines largely unimpeded by lofty vegetation, suddenly, and very unexpectedly, we enter a forest of mature trees, hundreds of them, thousands of them, tens of thousands of them, all the same size and shape, all defoliated, each extensively pruned but with new shoots shooting from the uppermost branches and into the sky, a forest of bare-limbed and obviously micromanaged trees . . . in the *desert!* Rey, my driver, says this is Sahuarita. Says this is where they grow the PE-cans. He's talking about Santa Cruz Farms, part of the Green Valley Pecan Company, the leading supplier of pecans to Europe. By Green Valley's own admission it's the world's largest irrigated pecan orchard. (It may also be one of the most historically intriguing properties in the pecan belt, as this land was once owned by Queen Wilhelmina of the Netherlands, who bought it from J. P. Morgan, Joseph Kennedy, and another investor who'd used the property to grow guayule, a rubber-containing shrub that thrives here in the deserts of the American Southwest.) Pecans in the desert! It almost doesn't make sense. After all, pecans originated in the Mississippi River valley of the South Central United States, where their long taproots tap into ample subterranean water tables, and where the trees are subjected sometimes to floods, and occasionally to droughts, but all in all to more or less regular rainfall. But the desert? The very word seems antithetical to the pecan tree. And it would be if not for Western-adapted pecan varieties such as Wichita or the Western Schley, the latter of which has been the most heavily planted pecan in the West in recent years.

Dr. Larry Stein, a horticulturalist at Texas A&M University, once told me that the "Western," which is how many refer to the Western Schley today, was developed because producers sought a pecan that had the quality of the original Schley—noted for its thin shell and high-quality kernel—that would thrive in the western growing area. It's been so successful that many consider the Western the "Cadillac" of pecans, which is saying something considering that industry insiders often refer to the pecan as the "Cadillac of nuts."

Shuck split heralds the "golden hour" in the annual cycle of pecan production. It is the result of a season's hard work, favorable environmental conditions, and tree varieties specially adapted to each pecan-growing region.

Equally important for southwestern agriculture is the miracle of irrigation, which, more than any other thing allows for the presence of this nut-producing oasis deep in the Sonoran Desert. Still, we're in the desert! And I can't help but think that these trees are so incongruous with their parched surroundings, such unlikely additions to the local flora, and located so far from the pecan's native range in present-day Arkansas, Louisiana, Oklahoma, and Texas that if I hadn't seen them myself I never would have believed they could grow here.

The trees appear to be carbon copies of one another. Stick figures, defoliated as they are. They're planted, it appears, in thirtyish-by-thirtyish (feet) spacing, in perfect rows, in military-grade ranks extending toward the mountains to the east and the copper mine to the west, as far as I can see. I've read estimates of over 100,000 trees. I've also read estimates of over 150,000 trees. In any case, this is a lot of work for any one army of pecan producers to take care of. But these aren't just tens of thousands of pecan trees. These are tens of thousands of very carefully managed pecan trees. Each tree, for example, has been topped and hedged, which are essentially industrial-strength pruning processes that remove unwanted limbs, allowing growers to raise more pecans than pecan wood. Topping and hedging provide for greater air ventilation in and among the trees, and pecan-producing sunlight penetration into the tree, and they allow for greater tree density per acre, all of which underscore the usefulness and value and growing popularity of these little gems of stratagems of pecan-growing strategies, which, ultimately, help farmers make better use of their precious pecan-producing acreage.

There are no leaves on the trees at this time of year, but in the summer, when each tree wears a thick canopy of foliage, Rey tells me that driving through this pecan forest offers a tangible benefit nearly as welcome, though not quite as refreshing, as an out-of-town neighbor's swimming pool. "In the summer," he says, "when it's really hot in Tucson, you can drive through here in the shade and it's much cooler."

"Like how much cooler?"

"Ten degrees."

No small relief when air temperatures hover at 105 degrees or more. I think of that old television commercial featuring cracked-soil settings and hot, sweaty hombres with dust-coated throats who smile in relief as they slick cold glasses of iced tea across their gritty foreheads before falling back, back into (*splash!*) . . . a swimming pool. Ahhhh. The Nestea plunge.

"Do many people around here work in the pecan industry?" I ask.

"A lot of people work in the pecans," he says.

I see none of these workers now as I gaze into this skeletal forest. To my surprise, there are lakes of standing water beneath the pecan trees. In some areas sprinklers are still spraying. In contrast to the surrounding desert, which is as dry as sunbaked leather, the ground here in the pecan forest is absolutely saturated. I wonder where the water comes from. Even the Santa Cruz River, which roughly parallels the highway, is dry.

At one point we stop at an intersection with another small highway. A few cars pass, and then we're underway once again, the cumbersome, lumbering old van carrying us south toward a US Border Patrol checkpoint and, just beyond, the international border with Mexico. But for now, we're still in Sahuarita. And for now, to my great surprise, we're still ensconced in the same forest of topped and hedged pecan trees. We've been in pecans for so long that the plane ride this morning into Tucson from Las Vegas now seems like something I did a long time ago. It seems we've spent the better part of our lives, Rey and I, driving through this immense forest of saturated ground and stick-figure trees. The only thing I can see in any direction, other than the mountaintops in the distance, other than Rey squinting through his glasses and out onto the sandpaper-dry highway baking in the Arizona sunshine, are pecan trees.

Regardless of where they're grown, there is one man who seems to know better than anyone else exactly where and how many millions of pounds of these nuts are being consumed. His name is Dan Zedan. Pronounced *zee-dan,* his name rhymes with how people in the southeastern United States pronounce the word *pecan.* His nut brokerage, Nature's Finest Foods, Ltd., based near Chicago, specializes in the marketing of almonds, walnuts, pistachios, and especially pecans, a crop he monitors closely. Zedan's news releases on pecans typically include statistics on things like annual crop volumes, exports, and, not surprisingly, Chinese demand.

Pecans were virtually unknown in China until recently, when organizations such as the Western Pecan Growers Association and the National Pecan Shellers Association began marketing here. It's fascinating to hear Zedan talk about the current generation's introduction to America's indigenous tree nut only a few years ago.

"When they were introduced to pecans, they called them funny walnuts because they'd never seen a pecan," he said. "They didn't know what it was. And they were afraid to taste them. They would touch the tips of their tongues to the pecans because they were afraid they would burn them."

Though initially reluctant, the Chinese found in pecans a nut that not only tastes good, but one that's also supremely nutritious. Today, they clamor for this iconic American food so much that there is, in the United States, as of March 2017, 60 million pounds of unsatisfied demand. That's because these 60 million pounds of US pecans are going to China.

It's true that China is experimenting with its own pecan-tree plantings, but considering that these nuts are not native to Asia, and given the country's often vertically oriented topography and a tendency to use its most productive farmland for staple crops such as rice, one wonders if pecans could ever be prolific producers here. Many believe the Chinese demand for pecans is so overwhelming that even if the trees thrived there the country could never produce enough to feed its own people. For this reason, China will probably always have to import most of its pecans.

In 2007 pecan popularity surged in China amid a reduced walnut crop that year. But as Zedan explained at the National Pecan Shellers Association meeting in Arizona ten years later, the pecan's competition from other tree nuts remains keen.

"Pecans are competing head-to-head with walnuts in 62 percent of distribution channels," he said, reporting from his lectern as he looked out at the audience. These were pecan men and women, the world's authorities in the production and processing of this crop, and yet Zedan was telling them about their own product's place in the domestic, and global, markets. Not only this, but Zedan frequently paused to correct figures on the PowerPoint slide deck accompanying his presentation, which might have been created only a few weeks earlier. Some of these

Growing demand for America's indigenous tree nut is pushing prices for pecans, such as this bag of Pawnees, higher all the time.

statistics had already changed, and despite having just traveled halfway around the world, to a pecan conference in South Africa and back again, and then from his home in the Midwest to the desert Southwest, he knew which figures had shifted and by how much.

"Currently, there's a three-dollar and fifty-cent price difference between pecans and walnuts," he continued. "And now pecans are competing with pistachios in the ingredient arena. Pistachio marketers decided to remove the shell from their product and sell the nuts as a cooking ingredient. It opened up a new channel."

The message? The pecan industry needs to figure out how to do the same, especially considering they're already at some disadvantage when compared to other nut crops. In a previous interview Zedan had told me that pecans are harder to sell than almonds or walnuts. He said almonds have been known for centuries in Europe, Africa, and Asia. "They've found almonds in the pyramids," he said. Pecans, by comparison, have been known outside the United States only for about the past twenty years. Although they've been promoted internationally in recent years, even here they're at a disadvantage. In 2016, for example, the US pecan industry spent $800 thousand in overseas promotion. By contrast, the almond industry spent $30 million.

In South Africa Zedan had spoken to growers about increasing demand for their own pecan crop. He said that over the past fifteen years South Africa has become the world's third-largest producer of pecans, behind only the United States and Mexico. Today, 98 percent of its annual crop goes to China. Evidently there is no domestic market for these pecans. Zedan's advice to the South African growers was to create one. "I told them, don't worry about supply," he said. "Demand is key. This ensures you'll be able to sell your crop in the future."

By all accounts it would seem that China's appetite for pecans is nearly insatiable—as is potentially, India's, if politicians can ever convince the Indian government to reduce its current 30-plus-percent tariff—so much so that growers around the world are focusing on getting their crop into this enormous nut-consuming nation. In doing so, domestic markets, such as those in the United States and South Africa, have often been neglected. As problematic as this has been, these deficiencies also present tremendous opportunities. There is certainly a need. The question is, who's going to fill it? This is one reason why so many are getting into the pecan business.

At the Arizona gathering Zedan told of meeting a woman a few weeks earlier who was very interested in becoming a pecan farmer. "She'd driven fourteen hours to the conference in South Africa so she could talk to me about growing pecans," he said. "She plans to plant them in Namibia."

(Author's note: In July 2018, the subject of exporting American pecans to China became a bit more complicated when the Trump administration announced the United States would place tariffs on hundreds of Chinese products such as medical devices and auto parts. Beijing retaliated with a 25 percent duty on imports of 545 American items, including many agricultural products. This has resulted in, at the time of this writing, a 47 percent tariff on American pecans exported to China. Long-term effects of this new tax are unclear, but for now pecan-industry leaders are working with the US Department of Agriculture on a relief program to support farmers impacted by these tariffs.)

The following is a transcript of my interview with Mike Adams of Royalty Pecan Farms of Texas, conducted March 2, 2017, only a few months after his appointment as chairman of the newly formed American Pecan Council:

How would you describe the current state of the US pecan industry?
Adams: The pecan is the only [commercialized] indigenous nut to the North American continent. Pecans have a great story to tell, and we in this industry have not done a very good job of telling our story.

This is part of our motivation in working with the FMO [federal marketing order]. We have a real passion for this commodity. The pecan is not necessarily like other trees, where you go from planting the seed in the ground and it not coming up true to the seed that's planted, to a food crop that's being grown in Texas and Oklahoma bottomlands naturally. When you take care of them, they really produce. The kernel is so healthy. We're just now discovering the health benefits of pecans. Native Americans used to follow the pecan harvest up and down rivers. They knew what we're only beginning to know. That little kernel is the accumulation of sunlight, water, the tree, and the environmental conditions, and we get to eat it. There have been attempts to export pecan trees to other countries, but they haven't been successful. All other tree nuts in the US have been imported, but the one indigenous nut here in the US is difficult to export. But it has lent itself to making a unique food commodity in our present-day situation and history.

I see the industry expanding or broadening from where we are. I don't think we're turning the ship around, but we will make more people aware of the pecan. The objective for the FMO is to increase demand for pecans. What this translates to is everyone up and down the chain, from growers, shellers, to consumers seeing a quality, steady supply of a food product that's not been consistently available in the past. This will be a springboard for the rest of the world to discover the goodness and taste of the pecan, broadening what was already started, and which has been kept going in a fairly stable supply situation. The FMO telling our story will help this.

Do you agree with the assessment that the domestic market presents the greatest opportunity for the pecan industry?

Adams: I think there are opportunities for both domestic and international growth. The primary marketing campaigns will be in the domestic market. MAP [Market Access Program] funding has helped increase demand worldwide, particularly in China. Some companies have been going into Europe, Middle East, Turkey. This effort had already begun with market access funds, we just didn't have any budget to address or concentrate a campaign on the domestic market. The FMO will fill this gap. International markets have been addressed to some extent within the past ten years. The domestic market has been neglected. We've rested on our laurels.

What's the number one priority for the American Pecan Council for the foreseeable future?

Adams: 1. Increasing demand for pecans. 1(a) will be collecting better data. We as an industry need better data on which to base our decisions. There's a real interest in gathering better data—how many growers, acres, estimates for crop predictions, carryover numbers, etc. We don't feel we have an objective number for our industry. Most published numbers we have now seem to have an agenda attached. We as a council want to dispel any agenda so when someone sees a number from the American Pecan Council, it has merit and weight. It's a real number. Marketing (domestic marketing to increase demand) will be our No. 1 priority. Data collection is 1(a).

Research and development and packaging are also necessary components.

Does the American Pecan Council reflect the interests and priorities of the US pecan industry?

Adams: The American Pecan Board (formed in 2013) is a group that promulgated the FMO. It supported federal hearings to get the FMO passed. The board spent in excess of three years on a listening tour, seeing what pecan stakeholders wanted in the FMO. So when we came back to the table with the USDA and composed rules, it was what we had heard the industry wanted. So anything being proposed within the American Pecan Council is the result of what the industry wants. This is not a Lone Ranger effort. The council represents the interest of all pecan stakeholders: growers, shellers, buyers, accumulators, consumers. We traveled across the country to hear what they had to say.

We weren't out selling. We were out listening. What we have today is the result of what we heard and learned from stakeholders.

Is this the most important point in the industry's history?
Adams: Without question. We have people in the same room who've never been in the same room before. We have a very fragile coalition today. We want the FMO to work on behalf of everyone. There's no question this is an historic moment for the industry. To bring everyone together, to seat a council from [heretofore] fractured interests of industry, that's historic. And we're committed to making it work. We have to. Every five years we have a continuance vote. Growers are the individuals who voted the FMO in. Every five years they can vote it out. Our constituency we're beholden to is the producers, growers. The [Marketing Order] law was written in 1937 to empower producers. Here we are so many years later trying to carry out this same purpose. Our constituency that we are beholden to is growers. This doesn't minimize the role shellers or handlers or accumulators play, but the continuance vote that voted it in has the option to continue or not. Look at the history of almonds, walnuts, etc. Growers passed the continuance vote by 90 percent. This is a high bar. We know when our vote comes around that growers trust us.

What is the biggest challenge for the pecan industry at this point?
Adams: We have many challenges in various segments of the industry. For growers, we need to continue planting trees and providing a consistent quality supply. That's the goal or focus of growers. Continue to put out a good product in a consistent supply so shellers can add value by cracking it and taking out a quality kernel. Shellers convert

the in-shell pecan to a kernel. Their challenge is quality control. They have a marketing function. Their goal should be continued cooperation with growers to prevent the kind of adversarial relationship there has been in the past.

Telling our story and getting the word out with some of the scientific research that we already have is another challenge. Marketing is certainly a challenge. Cooperation among all segments to share data so we have objective data everyone has confidence in is another challenge. Also, continued communication to our stakeholders. If we don't get the word out about what we're doing, and how, and being open with all our efforts, we'll be shortsighted. We have to keep our folks that have a stake informed.

How does the US pecan industry develop into a cohesive, uniform brand ("US pecans") after operating independently for so long?

Adams: I think it will be called American pecans. We did a study and the word "American" seemed to have a more universally positive connotation. We found that the term "US" does not always have a favorable connotation. Going forward, our product will be known as the American pecan because the distinctive nature of the term "American" is a plus. As far as branding, I think this is the brand we're talking about. There will still be state or regional efforts, which is not at all untoward what we're trying to do. There are regional differences with regard to specific pecan varieties, the climate in which pecans are grown in, etc. There is a place for regional and state branding. I don't think these labels are antagonistic. They will complement one another.

What's the biggest opportunity for the pecan industry?

Adams: Telling its story and taking or building on what's already known. The current research going on that's exciting. Once published, those kinds of stories will continue to come out. I don't think we know. We've just scratched the surface about the pecan's goodness. Telling our story, differentiating the pecan as a tree nut. In some parts of the world it's considered a walnut. The Chinese language only recently developed a word for pecan. There's nothing to compare it to in some countries. Separating it apart as a distinctive tree nut is part of our task because it is considered in many parts of the world a walnut, and that's understandable because if pecans have not been in that population, they have nothing to put it up against or compare it to. Like reading about dinosaurs. We have nothing to compare it to. Also, there's lots of opportunity to communicate the pecan's health benefits.

Is there still a part for China to play in the future of US pecans? Or has the pecan industry benefited all it can from the Chinese?
Adams: I think there's a huge upside, and it has to do with the number of consumers in China and the number of Chinese moving into the middle class with discretionary income, who can afford pecans. It's known as an upscale, high-end nut that costs more. This market is still large. The Chinese grow walnuts but not pecans. They may have a few trees, but there's not a supply coming from within their country like there is with walnuts. We don't have a competing supply with pecans. Mexico, South Africa produce some. But most [80 percent] of the world's supply comes from the North American continent.

What's the ratio of improved to native pecans in the annual US crop?
Adams: The annual harvest is 80/20 improved to native [80 percent improved to 20 percent native] pecans. Native pecans are grown with little input and in many cases no cost, whereas improved variety have a large cost over the course of the growing season. If prices are good, growers will pick up native pecans, but they won't when prices are down. Fifty or sixty years ago, the percentage of natives to improved was 40/60. Now it's more like 20/80.

> There's a distinctive nature to the native pecan. It has a higher oil content, a richer flavor. It's smaller with a thicker shell. These are unique qualities. I think right now the Chinese want larger nuts, but I think if we got native nuts into China, it would be just as preferred. The Chinese already have their own native hickory, a small nut like our native pecans.
>
> Native pecans have been around longer than improved [varieties], and they'll stay around longer than the improved varieties. They're here because of natural selection. They're survivors. Survived hundreds of years, and they'll be around. With improved pecans, if you don't manage, it will go away. But native, through natural selection, there's a reason it's there.

After nearly a year of floods and ebbs and missed opportunities, I finally got the chance to see Oklahoma's champion pecan tree early one morning in March 2017. Justin Roach, biologist at the Tishomingo National Wildlife Refuge, drove me out to the river bottom where the great tree stands along with several other large, distinguished pecans. Justin is a kind and generous man who is extremely knowledgeable about the area's flora and fauna, especially Tishomingo's wealth of bird life. I'm most grateful for the time he shared with me.

Climbing out of his pickup truck, I stood there admiring the champion pecan for some time. About twelve or fourteen feet off the ground, in a notch formed by a branch stemming from the main trunk, was a large log, a piece of debris from the historic 2015 flood. As incredible as this was, Justin told me the waters had actually crested four or five feet higher than this. Viewing it from the ground it appeared that half of the tree had been submerged in the floods, though in reality only about one-fourth of the eighty-two-foot pecan had been underwater. Still, that's eighteen or twenty feet of water, and the tree had spent many weeks so submerged. Yet it seemed healthy and solid.

I walked around its behemoth trunk again and again, wondering about its age, trying to entice Justin into hazarding a guess while telling myself that we'd probably never know and that its age didn't matter anyway. It was a grand old tree, and despite the countless weather extremes it had faced in its long life, it was still standing, still showering the ground with pecans each autumn. Charles Rohla calls our native pecan trees "survivalists," citing their ability to endure the worst weather and somehow maintain their productivity while living to be hundreds of years old. Oklahoma's champion pecan is certainly this. Still, I worry that the powerful winds that blow across our fields and through our forests will eventually prove too much for the soggy river-bottom soil that holds it and will topple the great tree, closing the book on the glorious story that its mammoth trunk and sprawling branches have shared with us for all these years. And I wonder, would anyone notice? Would anyone care?

The current clamor for jumbo-sized, easily cracked pecans has caused me to question our perceived value of pecan trees. What is a pecan tree worth? And with a market that demands the largest, most easily accessed pecan kernels, what is a wild tree, one that produces fewer and smaller nuts, worth?

In viewing the Oklahoma champion pecan, and in experiencing the splendor of other mammoth-sized wild trees, it seems to me that these living windows to the past are worth the years that nature has taken to produce and grow them. They are worth the time it takes us to find and admire them. And as a nation, as a society that prizes this most American of nuts, we must agree that they are worth the effort it takes to protect them. In one sense they're no different from the American bison or bald eagle. They're part of our ecological heritage and identity, and considering the vital role they've played in our country's history, perhaps we'll realize that wild pecan trees deserve a place in our future as well, even if most of today's pecans are produced by trees propagated by human hands rather than Mother Nature's.

As I stood back and admired the gentle giant overlooking this vast river bottom, I noticed the tree's trunk featured a deep crack, a stress fracture perhaps, developed from the immense strain of holding each of the tree's massive upper branches in place through many decades of wind and sun and rain. And yet the giant pecan seemed unaffected. Like the nation whose soil has anchored this grand old tree for all these years, and as with the pecan industry itself, whose stakeholders are today beginning to work together after a long period of division, time had proven the Oklahoma champion pecan tree's resilience and declared it a survivor.

Later, as we climbed into the pickup to leave, Justin pointed to another large pecan tree in the distance which he said contained an owl's nest. I couldn't see it, so he took out a tripod and spotting scope. Once he had the nest in focus I stepped up to the optic, peered into the viewfinder, and found myself face to face with an adult great-horned owl and a surprisingly large—and obviously well-fed—owlet. The mother's ear tufts appeared to be three inches tall, and they fluttered in the warm Oklahoma breeze as she casually observed us through sleepy eyes. The youngster beside her appeared more intrigued, however, and peered down at us from the safety of its elevated nest, some sixty feet or more off the ground.

The owls had the best view around. Their nest looked out over the expansive river bottom with its lush blanket of winter wheat, Cumberland Pool in the distance, and just to their left, the spectacular sight of Oklahoma's greatest pecan tree.

—10—

Home of the Pecan Festival

It is early November, and I'm in the Country Store in downtown Colfax, Louisiana, gazing at the cascading bushels of children's artwork gracing the wall. It's Friday afternoon, the first day of the Louisiana Pecan Festival, and tiny Colfax is humming with activity. People are entering the store to get out of the hot sun—air temperatures today hover in the mideighties, with humidity levels rivaling those inside a pot of brewing Community Coffee—or to purchase fresh pecans or pecan candy or pecan pie or pecan oil or most any other pecan-related item you can imagine. A small group of locals stands nearby, jawing with one another and laughing, as a baby's breath of breeze blows into the store, providing a moment of relief from the Louisiana heat.

The artwork is arranged by grade level, with blue-ribbon winners on top, beneath which are the second-place entries with their red ribbons, and so on down the wall. The winning image for the fifth-grade division depicts a large Ferris wheel rotating beneath a bright blue sky, while in the foreground is a pecan tree with nuts scattered beneath it on the ground. It's an image created in the realist tradition for it replicates the scene outside the Country Store: a frenetic midway bisected by railroad tracks, one side featuring a grove of carnival rides, including roller coasters and a Ferris wheel, and numerous others, and on the other side two quarter-mile lanes of vendor booths offering everything from mayhaw jelly to fresh gumbo to hand-polished duck calls, wildlife artwork, cypress furniture, boudin balls, fried alligator, leather belts, and certainly lots of pecans. Beyond Vendor's Alley, along Eighth Street in downtown Colfax, huge logs have been situated for public seating. Crowds of men, women, and children with strings of purple and gold beads around their necks, many wearing LSU Tigers T-shirts and baseball caps, stroll along the street and sidewalk, congregating in front of the Pecan Festival Office or the main stage, where a song from the 1980s-era rock band Poison blares from the speakers, and where, just a few hours earlier, the Pecanettes—a group of perky, junior-high girls in glittery green blouses and sleek black pants—delighted the crowd with their dancing, and also where, tomorrow at noon, many of the 80,000 attending this year's festival will turn their attention to the highly anticipated presentation of the Louisiana Pecan Festival Queen. The Pecan Festival Queen is selected from contestants across Louisiana. She reigns over the festival and serves as the official ambassador for Louisiana's pecan industry.

Until then, and tomorrow morning's Grand Parade, I have time to visit with some of the locals and learn more about pecans, which here in central Louisiana seem as abundant as anywhere I've visited in the pecan belt. In fact, on the thirty-minute drive down from Natchitoches earlier in the afternoon, I was taken with the acres of scattered pecan trees and orchards gracing the surrounding Red River lowlands and crowding the roadsides, where I noticed a couple of men crawling around on their hands and knees, filling large white buckets with these nuts.

The sign welcoming visitors to Colfax features the tagline, "Home of the Pecan Festival." As I parked my car beneath a couple of large pecan trees and got out to take a photo, I noticed the grass around the sign was littered with nuts. They seemed to be almost everywhere, which is fitting for a town that plays host to an event that *USA Today* recently included in its list of the nation's ten best fall harvest festivals.

I love Louisiana and always have, which is one reason I chose to visit this state's pecan festival. The other reason is that Louisianans seem to know better than anyone else how to celebrate *every*thing. I didn't know what exactly to expect from the Louisiana Pecan Festival, but I knew it wouldn't disappoint. And that's because of the friendly and spirited people I knew I'd meet. After all, while pecans are central to this annual festival, they're only one of the many reasons why the event earned a place on *USA Today*'s Top 10 list.

Back in the Country Store, I meet a woman named Juli, who delights in telling me about her Kiowa pecans, which are available already shelled or as pre-cracked, in-shell nuts. Juli tells me she works as an accountant by day, but by the time the pecan festival rolls into town each November, she is ready to get out of the office and visit with people.

"I've already talked to two television stations so far today," she tells me. "And the festival is just getting started. Better than last year, though. I'm a hundred pounds lighter this year," she says with a smile.

We talk about her pecans for a few minutes as customers file back and forth through the Country Store, talking, laughing, buying pecan cookies and pralines and pies. Juli offers me a sample, removing a pecan from a mesh bag. It's a Kiowa, large and heavy, with its light-colored shell already cracked for easy access to the goodness within. I peel away the remnants of the shell and behold the giant kernel, both halves intact. It is sweet and delicious.

Eventually talk gets around to the pecan oil on the next table. Juli smiles as she explains its health benefits—low in saturated fats, high in heart-healthy polyunsaturated and monounsaturated fats, and with a smoke point exceeding that for nearly all other cooking oils. Then she mentions that it's even better for the skin.

"I use pecan oil on my face and arms, and look at me," Juli says, turning her face side to side, earrings dangling. Her skin is smooth and possesses a healthy sheen. "I've been using it for four years, and it's made all the difference," she says. "I'm seventy, but people tell me I look like I'm fifty. What do you think?"

"I would have never guessed you're seventy," I say.

"Feel my arms," she says, holding out her arm and twisting her wrist. "It's the pecan oil. I have a friend who uses it on her cuticles. She even massages it into her scalp. Makes her hair grow about that much every two weeks," she says, holding her hands about twelve inches apart.

Juli tells me she uses pecan oil on her fingers as well. She says they get dry from handling paper for many hours each day. Then she smiles and tells me it was a different kind of paper she held way back in the 1960s.

"I saw Jimi Hendrix and Janis Joplin at the Monterey Pop Festival," she says with a grin. "I really *lived* the sixties. That was the best music ever."

I thank Juli for the sample and buy a bag of her Kiowa pecans. Then, before leaving the Country Store, I return to look at the wall of children's artwork, where another picture catches my eye. In the center is an enormous pecan pie. Orbiting the pie are numerous objects and accompanying captions, which read: "pecan sun," "pecan tree," "pecan table cloth," "pecan pizza," "pecan ice cream," "pecan pie milkshake," and "pecan earth." This entry won second place, but had I been judge, I might have given it the blue ribbon because it seems to capture the very essence of the pecan festival.

Across the street, after stopping by the pecan festival office for an official T-shirt and poster, I notice a store with a two-part sign. One part reads, "Fogleman's Pecans." The other, "Fogleman's Fishing Tackle." I walk inside and am greeted by a mature, easygoing gentleman who smiles and encourages me to peruse the aisles of fishing gear, which are cordoned off with a strand of bright yellow police crime-scene tape. They're accessible only through the aisle closest to the cash register. With 80,000 visitors expected for the weekend, Mr. Fogleman is just being prudent. After all, he could have closed his doors, like the pharmacy just down the street, with its old-fashioned soda foundation, the kind I remember from my childhood, the kind I wish I could take in and experience, but which, regrettably, is of no service to anyone at the moment.

The gentleman at Fogleman's introduces himself as Alvin and proceeds to tell me he is an Eagle Claw (fishing hooks) representative of fifty years' standing. "I used to live in Dallas," he says. "Had the whole state of Texas."

Most of the store seems to be stocked with fishing tackle. On the counter near the cash register are several bags of pecans, both shelled and unshelled varieties. Also, there is a rack nearby on which are a dozen or so jars of Fogleman's Cane Syrup.

"How's this cane syrup?" I ask.

"Oh, man," Alvin says. "That's the best stuff. You can put it on pancakes," he says. Now he smiles and adds, "It's really good on biscuits."

When I ask Alvin about his pecans, he points to a small, gray-haired woman behind the counter: his wife, Becky. She tells me they're Shawnee and Choctaw pecans. She also tells me her Desirables didn't produce this year.

"We had a dry summer," she says. "And it was dry into the fall. There were cracks in the soil out there an inch wide until just the other day. We got ten inches of rain."

"Had water in the store here," Alvin says from across the room.

Becky asks where I'm from, and when I tell her she asks if I live anywhere near Moore, where the tornadoes struck. I tell her no, that I live on the opposite side of Oklahoma City.

"There was one tornado that tracked that way just a few years ago," she says. "It went up into Edmond."

"I remember," I tell her.

"I love watching the Weather Channel," she says. "I love their reruns of severe weather events."

I ask her if she enjoys eating pecans. She tells me yes, if they're fresh. She says she keeps some in the refrigerator and grabs a handful for a snack. I drift over to a display case filled with pocketknives as Alvin moves behind the fishing counter and takes a seat. When I ask him how many pecan trees he has, it is Becky who responds. She's still standing behind the pecan counter across the room. "We have ten acres," she says. "Two hundred and twenty trees."

Some customers enter the store, and one approaches Becky's counter to make a purchase. I ask Alvin how many pounds of pecans they produce annually. He can't recall and tells me he doesn't worry about it. He says Becky takes care of that and that he handles the cracking and shelling. And the fishing.

"The fishing's pretty good around here?" I ask.

"Oh, man," he says. "We have great bass fishing. And bream. I was out just the other day catching bream that big. I was using live crickets."

Eventually I decide on a bag of shelled pecans and at Alvin's insistence a jar of cane syrup, made with real Louisiana sugar cane. As I say goodbye and head toward the door, Becky calls out from behind the pecan counter. "Now we'll have someone to pray for when we hear about tornadoes in Oklahoma."

"And I'll do the same when I hear about hurricanes down here," I tell her.

"We get tornadoes, too," she says.

I walk to my car and climb inside for the drive back to Natchitoches. As I leave Colfax for the evening, I notice a small sign that says, "Fogleman's Fishing Tackle." It's tacked to a pecan tree.

The next morning the Grand Parade begins promptly at ten. It's warm and overcast, but as the minutes tick by the clouds gradually give way to the sun. Short barricade fences have been situated along the streets of Colfax, and the crowd lines the parade route, in some places several rows deep. There are families gathered in lawn chairs, sitting around ice chests and charcoal grills. There are barbecue smokers smoking and smelling of hickory and pork. A woman walks a baby goat on a dog's leash. Another woman has ridden her lawn tractor to the parade. Her dog rests at her feet. Teenagers dart around the periphery on four-wheeled ATVs. And as I check the settings on my camera, a young mother and her two boys move up to the fence beside me. One of the boys has a net, which I immediately understand is not for catching butterflies. People are laughing and smiling and waving and chatting with one another. It's Saturday, the second day of the Louisiana Pecan Festival, and everyone has come out to see Colfax at its best. According to the festival president, Amber Garcia, whom I interviewed a few days earlier, it's the year's biggest event for Grant Parish.

"It's a community booster," she told me. "The festival is one of the largest sources of tax revenue for the parish, which is very rural, with limited businesses. The parish gets 20 to 30 percent of its annual revenues just from these three days."

When I asked Ms. Garcia why the community celebrated pecans rather than, say, cotton, she said that pecans are native to the area and that there are an abundance of trees along the Red River. "Pecans are no farmer's staple crop around here," she said, "but they bring in extra money. Everybody is a farmer of pecans because everybody has pecan trees in their yard or on their property. This time of year lots of people are out picking pecans after work or on weekends. They use the money they get for Christmas or Thanksgiving."

If the Grand Parade is any indication, Christmas may have arrived early this year. Showers of candy rain down on the crowd pressing against the fence. As a pickup truck rolls by out on the street, the young boy beside me holds out his net. A couple of Tootsie Rolls fall inside. I add to this the roll of SweeTARTS I've just caught. I tell myself pecans would be a nice party favor, but the crowd here already has pecans. They're everywhere. Besides, they're too valuable to fling into the crowd. So it's candy, all sorts of candy, and a lot of it. Each float, each pickup truck, tractor, van, bicycle, ATV, and participating pedestrian party is the source of a new shower of sugar-sweet candy.

A van decorated in LSU purple and gold drifts past. Candy blasts out of its open doors and windows as the LSU tiger mascot whips the crowd into a frenzy. Now come the Pecanettes, preceded by four Pecanette groupies riding in a 1950s-era Ford Fairlane convertible, music pumping from the speakers, and the Pecanettes, in their glittering green blouses, stepping and dancing and leading the crowd in spirit and cheer as candy falls from the sky. The kid beside me makes another catch with his net. I grab a piece of candy as it flies through the air just above my head and add to his haul. He quickly thanks me and prepares for the next attraction moving our way. It is a white Ford pickup truck carrying the Louisiana Pecan Festival Grand Marshall and an entourage that fills the vehicle's front and back seats, and most of its bed. All appear to be accomplished candy throwers, and throw candy they do. Each shower sends the crowd scrambling to pick up the sweet gifts flying through the air and sliding across the street.

And now come the queens, the Louisiana Pecan Festival Queen, and her Teen Queen, gliding down the street on a shiny, gold-tinseled float as the purple clouds part, letting the sun shine through, down onto the queens' crowns, which twinkle and glint. They are toting, not candy, but beads, necklaces of gold and purple and green beads that the queens and their entourages cram into their hands, aim, and fire into the crowd, sending whirling loops of Louisiana love through the air and into the grasping hands beyond the barricade. As the Louisiana Pecan Festival Queen glides by, I'm left with the image of a pecan tree on the back side of her float, the queen hovering above it.

The Louisiana Pecan Festival Queen, selected each year from contestants across the state, graces the festival's Grand Parade and serves as ambassador for Louisiana's pecan industry.

Now a marching band comes marching by, and a white pickup truck representing a candidate for sheriff whose truck-bed entourage showers the crowd with waves and smiles and candied rain, and now a band of sheiks from Alexandria, Louisiana, whose sword-wielding leader wears a beaded gold turban that glints and glows in the sunshine. Here comes agriculture and forestry commissioner Mike Strain riding in back of an old Chevrolet pickup truck, and along with his derby-hatted companion, flinging miniature Frisbees into the crowd. He is followed by a dance troupe for the ages, a battalion of ballerinas and tappers and high-steppers from Vicki's Dance Centers strutting down the street in their purple-and-black attire, keeping audiences enthralled and themselves jumping to the thumping beats pumping from the speakers. The dancers are trailed by the Cajun navy, whose armada is captained by a fleet of long-legged ladies flinging life preservers to those in candy-deprived distress, and this is followed by none other than Governor John Bel Edwards's very own campaign team, flinging purple plastic cups from the campaign trailer. Audience members raise their hands and shout, "Over here! Me, me, me! Throw me something!" as the American flag waves overhead and the fleur-de-lis festoons the float's flanks. Next comes a convoy of tractors, followed by the Louisiana Pecan Festival's Toddler Miss, a gold-crowned cutie looking out from the bed of a Dodge pickup truck. The tractors are followed by a peloton of whimsical-looking bicycles with fat tires and chopper handles and sissy bars, who insist on riding their two-wheeled machines in every possible direction except for a straight line. The cyclists are followed by more tractors, and by Miss Merry Christmas and the Christmas Belles of Natchitoches, Louisiana, showering the season's sweetest greetings on a crowd seemingly from all walks of life, as racially and socioeconomically varied, and as age- and occupationally diverse, as any I've seen anywhere in the pecan belt: a microcosm of America.

According to the US Census Bureau, Grant Parish, with a population of 22,336 as of July 1, 2017, has a median household income of about $40,000 and a per capita income of roughly $18,000. The real assets in this rural part of the state are the area's fields and forests and bayous and pecan trees—its natural beauty—and also its friendly and hospitable people, including the woman standing beside me, who is watching the parade with her two young children. Upon realizing my affinity for Kit Kat bars, and my inability to catch one of these candied treasures, she rakes through her son's bulging net of sweets, finds a Kit Kat single and offers it to me. As two years of wandering across the pecan belt had suggested, and as the festival had for the past two days shown me, pecans reflect so much of what's great about America. They are distinctive. They're wonderfully diverse. They're deeply rooted in our history and perhaps suggestive of our future, given their adaptability.

Cultivated trees dominate today's pecan industry. Yet, in certain areas, native pecans remain an ecologically and economically significant component of this industry despite the development over the past century of hundreds of new varieties and an effort to plant them exponentially. In their natural strongholds wild pecans often reflect the health of their surrounding environments (and human communities), making them something of an indicator species. Where they've been introduced, pecan trees enhance the viability of local economies. One is symbolic of American grit and tenacity, while the other captures our vision and ingenuity. Both types of trees are important to today's pecan industry, whose future prosperity, like that of our nation, would seem to rest largely with its constituent members and their willingness to stand together in recognition of inherent commonalities.

Appendix

The following are brief descriptions of twenty-five USDA-indexed pecan cultivars. There are over one thousand named pecan varieties. Those listed here include both historic and modern cultivars. Yield figures are approximate and often differ from one source to another. On paper, the differences between each cultivar may appear slight or even superficial, but these variances often amount to something significant in the orchard.

Barton: Released in 1953. Originated by crossing the pecan varieties Moore and Success. Forty-eight nuts to the pound; 57 percent kernel. A precocious and prolific cultivar with very good scab resistance.

Burkett: This is an old variety, introduced in 1911, and widely used as seed stock for the western growing region. Burkett has been used in the breeding of Apache and Comanche, and is noted for its round-shaped nuts.

Caddo: This variety was developed in Georgia in the 1920s as a cross between Brooks and Alley. A highly distinctive pecan, with a shape that tapers into fine points on either end of the shell, Caddo is considered precocious and produces high-quality nuts with excellent shelling characteristics.

Cape Fear: Cape Fear was developed in North Carolina as an open-pollinated Schley seedling. A precocious and prolific cultivar producing well-filled nuts, it has shown good scab resistance in many, but not all, areas of the pecan belt, although it is highly susceptible to bacteria leaf scorch. This variety has a tendency to overbear at maturity, which can reduce nut quality if measures aren't taken to reduce the tree's crop load during summer.

Choctaw: Originated in Texas in 1946 by L. D. Romberg of the USDA, Choctaw was developed as a controlled cross between Success and Mahan. Released in 1959, this variety is elliptically shaped with a 58 percent kernel. The USDA notes that Choctaw is prolific and resistant to scab in most locations outside Louisiana, though it cautions that this variety requires close management in order to produce to its potential.

Desirable: One of the most popular cultivars in southern orchards in recent decades, Desirable is a prolific variety, producing large, well-filled nuts that bring some of the highest prices in the pecan market. The USDA notes that Desirable (thirty-eight nuts per pound; 54 percent kernel) bears in six years, though it's highly susceptible to scab. For this reason, many extension agents are now recommending other, newer cultivars featuring greater scab resistance.

Elliott: Elliott produces a small, teardrop-shaped pecan of excellent quality. This and its resistance to scab have endeared it to many growers in Georgia, where it excels. It tends to leaf out early in the year, however, which makes it susceptible to late freezes. For this reason, Elliott is recommended for homeowners and growers in the Deep South.

Forkert: Developed in Mississippi in the early twentieth century, ostensibly from a cross between Success and Schley, Forkert produces a large pecan, yielding about forty-nine nuts per pound. Though not considered precocious, this variety is noted for its high nut quality.

Gloria Grande: W. W. Watson, of Watson's Pecanwood Nurseries in Orangeburg, South Carolina, discovered Gloria Grande as a seedling in 1920. Watson is said to have named this cultivar after Gloria Swanson, his favorite actress. It produces a medium-sized nut. Though not precocious, Gloria Grande is noted for its resistance to scab.

GraKing: Originated in Hugo, Oklahoma, as a chance seedling grown from Texas seed, GraKing was introduced in the late 1950s. A large pecan that's well suited to the in-shell market, it yields approximately thirty-five to forty nuts per pound.

Imperial: This seedling originated from unknown parentage and was introduced in 1962. The plant patent was issued in 1963 and assigned to Aldridge Nursery in Von Ormy, Texas. Imperial is a large nut with a classic, elliptical shape, thirty-two to the pound, with a 56 percent kernel, golden in color.

Jackson: A controlled cross between Success and Schley, Jackson originated in Mississippi in 1917. It's been called "Thirty-Three" for the fact that it often takes as few as thirty-three nuts to form one pound. The USDA describes this variety as elliptic with obtuse apex and rounded base, and producing a 52–56 percent kernel, rectangular in shape, and golden to light brown in color.

Kanza: A newer variety, Kanza was developed from a cross between Major and Shoshoni and released in 1996. It was designed to be an excellent producer in the northern growing region and is noted both for its cold tolerance and excellent scab resistance. Kanza produces a smaller, high-quality nut.

Kiowa: Originating in Texas during the 1950s and released in 1976, Kiowa produces a large, high-quality pecan, well-suited to the in-shell market. Kiowa is a precocious cultivar, and it cross-pollinates well with Desirable. It lacks cold hardiness, however, and is susceptible to scab.

Mahan: Mahan is an old variety noted for producing very large, thin-shelled pecans. Used extensively for breeding, Mahan has figured into the development of cultivars such as Choctaw, Wichita, Kiowa, and Harper. The USDA considers Mahan precocious and prolific but cautions that it's highly susceptible to scab.

Maramec: Originated as an open-pollinated Mahan seedling by Emma Charlton of Maramec, Oklahoma and introduced in 1969, Maramec is a large, oblong pecan yielding forty-four nuts to the pound. Considered precocious, though susceptible to scab, this variety is still grown in Oklahoma.

Mohawk: Mohawk originated in Texas in 1946 from a cross between Success and Mahan. It was released in 1965. This variety produces large pecans, well-suited to the in-shell market. It's considered prolific and "very precocious," according to the USDA, though it's susceptible to freezes and, in some parts of the South, to scab.

Oconee: Oconee originated in the 1950s from a cross between Schley and Barton and was released in 1989 for use in the southern portions of the US pecan belt. Featuring moderate scab resistance, Oconee produces a large pecan with high kernel quality and a thin, easily cracked shell.

Pawnee: Pawnee originated in 1963 from a cross between Mohawk and Starking Hardy Giant. This variety produces a large, high-quality nut, and with its tendency for early maturing—which allows growers to get their crop into the market early, for the best prices—it's becoming extremely popular across many areas of the US pecan belt.

Podsednik: A massive pecan, one of the largest cultivars, yielding twenty-two nuts per pound, Podsednik originated in Arlington, Texas, in 1968 as a seedling planted by Robert Podsednik. It is often grown today as a novelty for its large pecans.

Schley: An old variety, Schley was developed from a seedling tree planted in 1881 in Mississippi and is one of the cultivars that helped establish the pecan industry in the southeastern United States. With its thin shell and oily, flavor-packed kernel, it has figured into the development of a number of pecan cultivars over the years, including Apache, Sioux, Cherokee, Cape Fear, and others. According to the USDA, Schley has long been considered the pecan industry's standard for nut quality.

Stuart: One of the oldest and most widely planted cultivars, Stuart is often used as the standard by which to measure other pecan varieties, although it produces a medium-sized nut of only marginal quality. It's susceptible to scab and lacks precocity.

Success: An older variety selected from a Mississippi orchard planted in the late 1800s, Success, with its high quality kernel, has been used in the development of such cultivars as Choctaw, Desirable, Mohawk, and Pawnee. It's susceptible to scab and shuck disorders, however.

Western Schley: The "Western," as it's often called, produces a long, thin-shelled nut of medium size. It's the most widely planted cultivar in the southwestern United States, where it has proven highly successful. Because of its susceptibility to scab, Western is recommended only for the West.

Wichita: Wichita originated from a cross between Halbert and Mahan. Considered precocious and prolific, this variety produces medium-sized, well-filled nuts. While not recommended for growers in the Southeast due its susceptibility to scab, Wichita is one of the most popular and successful varieties in the Southwest, where this fungus is not a concern.

Bibliography

Ackerman, Frank, and Elizabeth Stanton. "The Last Drop: Climate Change and the Southwest Water Crisis." Stockholm Environment Institute. 2011. http://www.sei-us.org/publications/id/371. Retrieved December 16, 2017.

Albala, Ken. *Nuts: A Global History*. London: Reaktion Books, 2014.

Andersen, P. C. "The Pecan Tree." University of Florida, Institute of Food and Agricultural Sciences. http://edis.ifas.ufl.edu/hs229#FOOTNOTE_2. Retrieved December 16, 2017.

Benning, Tom, and Katie Leslie. "'Other Nuts, They Fear Pecans': Texas Growers Turn to Ted Cruz for Bigger Slice of Export Pie." *Dallas Morning News*, October 26, 2017.

Betts, Edwin Morris, ed. *Thomas Jefferson's Garden Book*. Thomas Jefferson Foundation, 2012.

Brensel, Mike. "Considering Cover Crops for Long-Term Soil Health and Sustainability." *Pecan South* 50, no. 7 (September 2017).

Brison, Fred. *Pecan Culture*. Austin: Capital Printing, 1974.

Bronner, Simon, ed. *Lafcadio Hearn's America: Ethnographic Sketches and Editorials*. Lexington: University Press of Kentucky, 2002.

Campbell, R. Douglas, and John H. Gordon, Jr. "Growing Pecan Trees in the North: Growing Pecan Trees in Minnesota or Canada? Yes You Can, with a Far-North, Native Species." *Mother Earth News*, March/April 1979.

Cardona, Claire. "Seguin Retaking the Pecan Crown: Nut Will Be the 'World's Largest.'" *San Antonio Express-News*, July 2, 2011. http://www.mysanantonio.com/community/article/Seguin-retaking-the-pecan-crown-1450043.php. Retrieved December 16, 2017.

Cockerham, Skyla, William Gorman, Niels Maness, and Jay Lillywhite. "Feasibility Assessment of Investing in a Pecan Oil and Flour Processing Facility Using New Extraction Technology." New Mexico State University, College of Agricultural, Consumer, and Environmental Sciences. Research Report 778.

http://aces.nmsu.edu/pubs/research/economics/RR778/welcome.html. Retrieved December 16, 2017.

Crosby, Gary. "Mississippi Pecan Pie." Reviewed by *Cash Box*, May 28, 1955. https://archive.org/stream/cashbox16unse_34#page/8/mode/2up/search/mississippi. Retrieved August 23, 2018.

De Voe, Thomas F. *The Market Assistant, Containing a Brief Description of Every Article of Human Food Sold in the Markets of New York, Boston, Philadelphia, and Brooklyn.* New York: Hurd & Houghton, 1867. https://books.google.com/books?id=2z4EAAAAYAAJ&printsec=frontcover&source=gbs_ge_summary_r&cad=0#v=onepage&q&f=false. Retrieved August 24, 2018.

Dorsey, George. *Traditions of the Caddo*. Lincoln: University of Nebraska Press, 1997.

Eaton, Elizabeth. "Future of S. Arizona Desert Farming and Development Floats on Water." *Arizona Sonora News Service*, December 9, 2016. http://arizonasonoranewsservice.com/in-the-arizona-desert-the-future-of-farming-and-development-floats-on-water/. Retrieved December 16, 2017.

Eichelberger, Julia, ed. *Tell about Night Flowers: Eudora Welty's Gardening Letters, 1940–1949*. Jackson: University Press of Mississippi, 2013.

Ferris, Marcie Cohen. *The Edible South: The Power of Food and the Making of an American Region.* Chapel Hill: University of North Carolina Press, 2014.

Fitzgerald, Deborah. *Every Farm a Factory: The Industrial Ideal in American Agriculture*. New Haven, CT: Yale University Press, 2003.

Francaviglia, Richard. *The Cast Iron Forest: A Natural and Cultural History of the North American Cross Timbers*. Austin: University of Texas Press, 2000.

Frazier, George. *The Last Wild Places of Kansas: Journeys into Hidden Landscapes.* Lawrence: University Press of Kansas, 2016.

Fuller, Andrew S. *The Nut Culturist: A Treatise on the Propagation, Planting, and Cultivation of Nut-Bearing Trees and Shrubs Adapted to the Climate of the United States, with the Scientific and Common Names of the Fruits Known in Commerce as Edible or Otherwise Useful Nuts.* New York: Orange Judd Company, 1904.

Garcia, Richard A. *Rise of the Mexican American Middle Class: San Antonio, 1929–1941*. College Station: Texas A&M University Press, 1991.

Gehlbach, Frederick. *Mountain Islands and Desert Seas: A Natural History of the U.S.-Mexican Borderlands.* College Station: Texas A&M University Press, 1981.

Gifford, John. "Are Americans About to Go Nuts for Pecans?" *Modern Farmer*. September 21, 2016.

Halbert, H. A. "The Constituents of an Ideal Pecan." *Pecans and Other Nuts in Texas*. Austin: Texas Department of Agriculture, 1908. TX document no.:

A900.7, B874, no. 2. https://babel.hathitrust.org/cgi/pt?id=hvd.32044107233017;view=1up;seq=5. Retrieved May 29, 2018.

Hargrove, James L., Diane K. Hartle, and Phillip Greenspan. *Health Benefits of Pecans*. St. George Island: Blue Heron Nutraceuticals, 2013.

Hearn, Lafcadio. *Creole Cook Book*. Gretna: Pelican Publishing, 1967.

Heat-Moon, William Least. *Blue Highways: A Journey into America*. New York: Back Bay Books, 1982.

Hedrick, U. P. *A History of Horticulture in America to 1860*. New York: Oxford University Press, 1950.

Holley, Joe. "Tough Nuts to Crack." *Texas Monthly*, March 1996.

Hume, H. Harold. *The Pecan and Its Culture*. Raleigh, NC: H. Harold Hume, 1910. https://archive.org/details/pecanitscultureoohume. Retrieved August 24, 2018.

Janick, Jules, ed. *Classic Papers in Horticultural Science*. Englewood Cliffs, NJ: Prentice-Hall, 1989.

Kolb, Carolyn. *New Orleans Memories: One Writer's City*. Jackson: University Press of Mississippi, 2013.

Lamberton, Ken. *Dry River: Stories of Life, Death, and Redemption on the Santa Cruz*. Tucson: University of Arizona Press, 2011.

Little, James A. *A Treatise on the Pawpaw*. Clayton: Orville G. Swindler, 1905. https://books.google.com/books?id=uJoaAAAAYAAJ&printsec=frontcover&dq=pawpaw&hl=en&sa=X&ved=0CDQQ6AEwAmoVChMImOygr9jkxgIVSjU-ChordQZK#v=onepage&q=pawpaw&f=false. Retrieved August 23, 2018.

Longworth, John W., Julie M. Valdez, Molly L. Magnuson, and Kenneth Richard. "New Mexico Water Use by Categories 2010." New Mexico Office of the State Engineer, Technical Report 54, October 2013. http://www.ose.state.nm.us/Pub/TechnicalReports/TechReport%2054NM%20Water%20Use%20by%20Categories%20.pdf. Retrieved December 16, 2017.

Manaster, Jane. *The Pecan Tree*. Austin: University of Texas Press, 1994.

Maril, Lee. *Crack & Crunch: Nuts in Fact and Fancy*. New York: Coward-McCann, 1945.

McCarthy, William Bernard. *Cinderella in America: A Book of Folk and Fairy Tales*. Jackson: University Press of Mississippi, 2007.

McEachern, George Ray. "Evaluating Pecan Problems." Texas A&M AgriLife Extension, October 20, 1995. https://aggie-horticulture.tamu.edu/fruit-nut/fact-sheets/evaluating-pecan-problems/. Retrieved December 16, 2017.

———. "Pecan chilling and delayed bud break." *Pecan South* 50, no. 3 (May 2017).

McFarland, J. Horace. *Getting Acquainted with the Trees*. New York: Macmillan,

1906. https://babel.hathitrust.org/cgi/pt?id=ncs1.ark:/13960/t1zc8439x;view=1up;seq=9. Retrieved August 21, 2018.

McWilliams, James. *The Pecan: A History of America's Native Nut*. Austin: University of Texas Press, 2013.

Menefee, Selden, and Orin Cassmore. *The Pecan Shellers of San Antonio: The Problem of Underpaid and Unemployed Mexican Labor*. Washington: Federal Works Agency, Work Projects Administration, 1940.

Metcalf, Woodbridge. *Introduced Trees of Central California*. Berkeley: University of California Press, 1968.

Moore, Andrew. *Pawpaw: In Search of America's Forgotten Fruit*. White River Junction: Chelsea Green Publishing, 2015.

Murray, Michael, N.D. *The Encyclopedia of Healing Foods*. New York: Atria Books, 2005.

Nuttall, Thomas. *A Journal of Travels into the Arkansas Territory, during the Year 1819. With Occasional Observations on the Manners of the Aborigines (1821)*. Whitefish, MT: Kessinger Publishing, 2010.

O'Sullivan, Robin. *American Organic: A Cultural History of Farming, Gardening, Shopping, and Eating*. Lawrence: University Press of Kansas, 2015.

Pauly, Philip J. *Fruits and Plains: The Horticultural Transformation of America*. Cambridge: Harvard University Press, 2007.

Phillips, George, Frank Gibbs, and Wilbur Mattoon. *Forest Trees of Oklahoma*. Oklahoma City: Oklahoma Planning and Resources Board, Division of Forestry, 1953.

Ree, Bill. "An Endless Treasure Trove of Information, Some Suggested Resources for Producers." *Pecan South* 50, no. 10 (December 2017).

———. "Twig Girdlers Frustrate Homeowners and Commercial Producers." *Pecan South* 50, no. 9 (November 2017).

Reed, C. A. The Pecan. Washington, DC: United States Department of Agriculture. Bureau of Plant Industry, Bulletin No. 251, 1912. https://archive.org/details/pecanooreed. Retrieved August 24, 2018.

———. "Pecan Culture; with Special Reference to Propagation and Varieties." Washington, DC: United States Department of Agriculture, Farmers' Bulletin 700. January 18, 1916.

Reid, Bill. "Northern Pecans: Climatic Adaptation." Northernpecans.blogspot.com. http://northernpecans.blogspot.com/2012/09/northern-pecans-climatic-adapation.html. Retrieved December 16, 2017.

Rohla, Charles. "Added Value in the Pecan Orchard." *Pecan South* 50, no. 4 (June 2017).

———. "Cross Pollination Is Essential for Pecan Production." Noble Research Institute. https://www.noble.org/news/publications/ag-news-and-views/2016/june/cross-pollination-is-essential/. Retrieved December 16, 2017.

Saikku, Mikko. *This Delta, This Land: An Environmental History of the Yazoo-Mississippi Floodplain.* Athens: University of Georgia Press, 2005.

Santerre, Charles. *Pecan Technology*. New York: Chapman & Hall, 1994.

Saxon, Lyle. *Fabulous New Orleans.* Gretna: Pelican Publishing, 1988.

Saxon, Lyle, Edward Dreyer, and Robert Tallant. *Gumbo Ya-Ya: Folk Tales of Louisiana.* Gretna, LA: Pelican Publishing, 1987.

Sherman, Joshua. "More Than Just a Dynamic Event, Shuck-Split Is Pecans' Annual Biochemical Ballet." *Pecan South* 50, no. 8 (October 2017).

———. "Transitioning from Flood to Micro Irrigation." *Pecan South* 50, no. 2 (April 2017).

Shiver, Art, and Tom Whitehead. *Clementine Hunter: Her Life and Art.* Baton Rouge: Louisiana State University Press, 2012.

Smith, J. Russell. *Tree Crops: A Permanent Agriculture.* New York: Harcourt, Brace, 1929.

Smith, Ron. "Pecan Groves Offer Profitable Options." Southwest Farm Press, May 20, 2008. http://www.southwestfarmpress.com/pecan-groves-offer-profitable-options. Retrieved December 16, 2017.

Smithwick, Noah. *The Evolution of a State: Recollections of Old Texas Days.* Independently published, 2016.

Starr, S. Frederick. *Inventing New Orleans: Writings of Lafcadio Hearn.* Jackson: University Press of Mississippi, 2001.

Stein, Larry. "Crop or Not, Make Your Native Timber Happier and Healthier." *Pecan South* 50, no. 5 (July 2017).

Stuart Pecan Company. *The Pecan, and How To Grow It.* Chicago: Women's Temperance Publishing Association, 1893.

United States Department of Agriculture. Crop Germplasm Research Unit. "Index of Pecan Cultivars." http://cgru.usda.gov/CARYA/PECANS/pecalph.htm. Retrieved December 16, 2017.

———. Economic Research Service. "Organic Market Overview." https://www.ers.usda.gov/topics/natural-resources-environment/organic-agriculture/organic-market-overview.aspx. Retrieved December 16, 2017.

———. National Agriculture Statistics Service. *2012 Census of Agriculture*—State Data. (Missouri, 33–34). https://www.agcensus.usda.gov/Publications/2012/Full_Report/Volume_1,_Chapter_1_State_Level/Missouri/st29_1_039_040.pdf. Retrieved December 16, 2017.

———. Natural Resources Conservation Service. *Carya illinoinensis.* https://plants.usda.gov/core/profile?symbol=CAIL2. Retrieved December 16, 2017.

Upson, Steve, Charles Rohla, James Locke, and Job Springer. *Pecan Production 101: Establishing and Managing an Improved Variety Pecan Enterprise in the Southern Great Plains.* Samuel Roberts Noble Foundation, Agricultural Division, 2012.

Wells, Lenny. *Pecan: America's Native Nut Tree.* Tuscaloosa: University of Alabama Press, 2017.

Wilson, James. *Clementine Hunter: American Folk Artist.* Gretna, LA: Pelican Publishing, 1988.

Wines, Michael. "Colorado River Drought Forces a Painful Reckoning for States." *New York Times*, January 5, 2014.

Woodroof, J. G., and Naomi C. Woodroof. "Pecan Root Growth and Development." *Journal of Agricultural Research* 49, no. 6 (September 15, 1934). https://naldc.nal.usda.gov/download/IND43968576/PDF. Retrieved December 16, 2017.

Zielinski, Sarah. "The Colorado River Runs Dry." *Smithsonian* Magazine, October 2010.

Acknowledgments

This book was made possible through the expertise and generosity of many individuals, including Charles Rohla, Brett Mason, Joanne Ryan, Kyle Troxell, Justin Roach, Dan Zedan, Collier Parker, Kelsey Jistel, John Pape, Tucker Hill, Teresa Barbre, Alex Willson, Diane Couch, Josh Grundmann, Janice Grundmann, Luis Cisneros-Zevallos, Mark Hamilton, Sally Harper, Laura Harper, Drew Kimmell, Joe Wilson, Bill Reid, Tom McPeek, Bill Ree, Larry Stein, Cindy Wise, Mike Adams, Alvin and Becky Fogleman, Amber Garcia, Michelle Muth Person, Beth Williams, Shanda Daniel, Daphne Schauber, Kristen Garcia, Mark Arena, Hilton Segler, Diane Jackson, Gwen Sparks, John White, Michael Seibold, Randi McSpadden, Jacque Knight, Stephen Norman, Trey Decker, Regina Berna, Joseph Moore, and Kevin Keys. I thank each of them for sharing with me their valuable time, as well as their considerable knowledge of pecans and the pecan industry. Also, I wish to express my gratitude to Kim Hogeland, editor at the University Press of Kansas, for supporting this project, and to George Frazier and Stephanie Anderson, whose wise and insightful feedback helped improve *Pecan America*. I'm most grateful for my wife, Ellen, and son, Jackson, who've always been my strongest and most ardent supporters and my greatest inspirations. I love you both. Thank you.

About the Author

John Gifford is a writer, essayist, photographer, and the author of several books, including *Wish You Were Here*, *The Sharks of Al Jubail*, and *Red Dirt Country*. His work has appeared in *Southwest Review*, the *Christian Science Monitor*, the *Saturday Evening Post*, and the *Atlantic*, and has been nominated for the Pushcart Prize and selected as "Notable" in *The Best American Essays*. He lives in Oklahoma.